BODY LANGUAGE SALES SECRETS

BODY LANGUAGE SALES SECRETS

How to Read Prospects and Decode Subconscious Signals to Get Results and Close the Deal

Jim McCormick and Maryann Karinch

CAREER
PRESS
Wayne, NJ

BODY LANGUAGE SALES SECRETS
Edited by Jodie Brandon
Typeset by Diana Ghazzawi
Cover design by Howard Grossman/12E Design
Printed in the U.S.A.

To order this title, please call toll-free 1-800-CAREER-1 (NJ and Canada: 201-848-0310) to order using VISA or MasterCard, or for further information on books from Career Press.

The Career Press, Inc.
12 Parish Drive
Wayne, NJ 07470
www.careerpress.com

Library of Congress Cataloging-in-Publication Data

CIP Data Available Upon Request.

To all the sales professionals
who use their expertise and professionalism
to serve their customers and clients.

··········

ACKNOWLEDGMENTS

First and foremost, we want to thank Gregory Hartley, whose knowledge about reading and using body language has been invaluable to us. You have served us as a mentor and a muse! Big thanks also to Jim Pyle, the guru of good questioning.

We want to offer sincere acknowledgment to the extraordinary sales professionals with whom we've had the privilege of working through the years. We value what we learned from you and appreciate your ability to sincerely serve your customers and clients.

As with any book about body language, we feel it only right to acknowledge the body of work of Paul Ekman; he has taught everyone in the field a great deal about understanding the connection between facial expressions and the truth of their feelings.

Two important colleagues also deserve special thanks for contributing to our evolution as professionals: Pete Pannes and Michael Carroll.

We also offer our deepest gratitude to the entire Career Press team: Ron Fry, Michael Pye, Adam Schwartz, Gina Schenck, Lauren Manoy, Laurie Kelly-Pye, Karen Roy, and Jeff Piasky.

··········

CONTENTS

PART 1

•••

THE FUNDAMENTALS

Yes.

In a sale, it's what you want to hear—and see—again and again. In this first section of the book, we familiarize you with key body language signals. You will know if you are headed toward *yes* or *no*. You will also get a keen idea of when you are facing indecision or deferral.

What can you do to improve your chances of seeing *yes*? How can you turn around a situation that seems bleak? For one thing, you can ask good questions. We explore what constitutes a good question as well as other conversation motivators.

As your prospect shares information, your listening skills help reinforce the rapport developing between you. With rapport comes the opportunity to build trust. You may encounter other responses along the way, though. Getting in the way of stronger rapport and trust could be disapproval, suspicion, confusion, distraction, embarrassment, or condescension. Moving you forward could be delight, comfort, hope, safety, certainty, and desire. You benefit from being able to spot all of them and know how to manage them.

Body language is more than expressions and movements, of course. Non-verbal communication encompasses vocal characteristics as well as utterances that are not words. It also includes how you present yourself and items that figures into your gesturing like a phone, a pen, or a rubber band.

Body language sales secrets are about both you and your prospect. You need to read other people at the same time that you maintain self-awareness. People are looking at you, too, and you want to project the attitude, demeanor, and emotions that are right for the moment.

Whatever you are selling—products, services, or ideas—as long as you come face to face with people, you will find valuable guidance and insights in the upcoming pages.

2

·········

BEYOND YOUR
COMFORT ZONE

Comfort zone: that place where you feel unthreatened and in control. In selling, you are outside it much of the time—if you're really good. An emotionally flat exchange with a prospect may project how stress-free you are, but that's as engaging as a first date with no spark. A certain amount of emotion helps establish and strengthen a connection; it's "good stress."

In selling, you are always pursuing a particular outcome (the order, the commitment, the contract), but being successful means accepting an uncertain path to your goal. That is the fun in selling: responding artfully and effectively to whatever comes your way during the sales process.

Let's start with the premise that you get a little amped when you're selling. In terms of body language, that means you are deviating from your baseline behavior; that is, you are being affected by stress, even if it's just a tiny amount. One of the results is that you unconsciously resort to a self-soothing movement. These movements range from the ordinary, like rubbing fingers together, to the strange and distracting, like wrapping a rubber band around a finger over and over again. (Yes, we've seen it.)

In this chapter, we begin by helping you identify your baseline and that of others. It's just as important that you know when you are deviating from your baseline as it is that you know when your prospect or customer is exhibiting signs of stress. We will also help you recognize what movements or vocal glitches you—and others you encounter—adopt in response to stress.

Baselining

A *baseline* is the composite of the movements and vocal expressions when you're in a relatively relaxed state. It is the way you act and speak in your comfort zone. Determining an individual's baseline is the first vital skill of reading and using body language.

A baseline and the factors contributing to it might change depending on the setting. For example, your style of relaxed speech and behavior might be different at home and at work. As a corollary, the topics that trigger an emotional response in these two environments might be different. At work, if a direct report says, "I don't want to do that," you might feel a wave of stress coming on. But if your 4-year-old child says, "I don't want to do that," it's just a sign of her budding independence.

Baselining is the skill set you rely on to pick up subtle variations in body language and tone of voice. Once you know what to look and listen for, you can detect changes that accompany stress of varying degrees. That ability gives you a high degree of control in your interaction with someone. It makes it possible for you to detect deception, mistrust, uncertainty, or any other emotion that could profoundly impact your interactions with someone.

There is no standard baseline for human beings any more than there is a standard hair or eye color. Sure, there may be significant similarities among people, but human beings can differ dramatically in how they behave when they are relatively relaxed. For example, we have probably all seen people who seem to go through life with their mouths open, that is, mouth-breathers. That's normal for them, whereas many of us wouldn't do that unless we were surprised or gasping for air. Similarly, some people have a tick or a quirky way of moving their hands. For other people, those would be signs of stress; for them, it's business as usual.

The basic steps to establishing someone's baseline are:

- Take in the overall picture. What's your impression of the person's state? Calm, agitated, uncomfortable, or anything else on the spectrum of emotions? Mentally put a label on it.

- If the person seems anything except calm and devoid of stress, this is not the moment to get a baseline. In Chapter 5, we cover ways to calm someone down (including yourself). In the meantime, here is a quick tip: Make an observation about something that's likely to be a "feel good" aspect of your prospect's life. If you notice that he has:

  ▷ A photo of a sailboat on his desk, ask, "Is that your boat?"

  ▷ Cufflinks that are little airplanes, ask, "Are you a pilot?"

  ▷ A suntan, remark, "Great tan. Vacation or golf?"

▷ A copy of *The Complete Works of William Shakespeare* on the bookshelf, ask, "Are you a Shakespeare buff?"

These are "yes" or "no" questions, so it's not as though you are asking the person to invest a lot of time in the answer. Even so, if the thing you noticed does represent an enjoyable part of the person's life, he'll probably give you at least a few sentences and will be more relaxed than before. Get started on determining the baseline.

- When you've concluded your subject is relatively relaxed, listen and observe to determine normal behaviors.

  ▷ Listen for fillers—that is, sounds such as "uh" and "um" and/or words such as "like" and "so" used frequently. If you hear them often when the person is in a calm state, then those fillers are a normal part of the person's expression.

  ▷ Listen to vocal pitch. If a woman with a mid-range pitch suddenly sounds like Minnie Mouse, then you've detected a deviation from baseline.

  ▷ Listen to vocal quality. A raspy or strident voice seems quite natural for some people, but for others, it indicates tension held in the vocal chords.

  ▷ Observe movements. In a moment, we'll explore some basic categories of movement that will help you sort out and interpret what you're seeing. For a baseline, however, the important thing is to take note of what movements are customary for the person.

▷ Observe the energy behind the movements. The amount of oomph behind a movement can be a matter of style, culture, age, or health. When establishing a baseline for someone, consider what seems to be the normal energy range for the person. In some cultures, for example, it is common to be effusive and demonstrative. In others, just a raised voice is considered out of place.

We have found eye movement to be a useful indicator of state-of-mind with many people and recommend baselining for that specifically. Your objective is to note whether the person looks up left or right when remembering something; he probably looks in the opposite direction when imagining something. These unconscious eye movements are called "eye accessing cues" or "visual accessing cues" because the eyes move toward the part of the brain responsible for vision, that is, the visual cortex, which is located in the back of the brain.

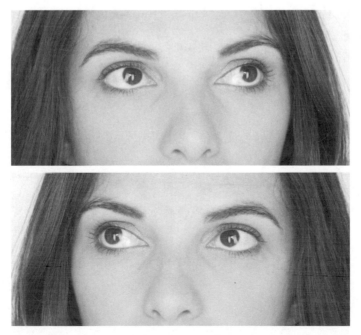

A question such as "How do you get from this office building to mid-town?" is an obvious visual memory question, just as "What do you think the surface of Jupiter is like?" is an imagination question. In the context of a sales meeting, however, you could probably evoke the response you're looking for by asking questions that focus on the task at hand. "How do you see your current system meeting your needs?" could get the person to move her eyes toward her memory side. "What's your vision of an ideal solution to this problem?" is essentially an imagination question, although the person may have thought so long and hard about the ideal solution that she's simply recalling the vision. You have your baseline on memory versus construct when you can identify the different directions, and you may need to ask several questions to get it. If you start you baselining with a "feel-good" subject such as those suggested previously, then you will almost certainly be able determine the recall side as your prospect describes his sail boat or how he landed at the Teterboro airport to escape a storm the previous weekend.

In sales, it's just as important for you know the elements of your baseline as it is to determine those of your prospect or customer. Even though that might seem easy, many of us are not as self-aware as we might think, however, so it helps to get input from a trusted colleague or friend.

Someone who has been around you a lot would be able to notice that you behave differently when the owner of the company or a high-dollar client is around, for example. You might think nothing has changed, but you've deviated from your baseline because some level of stress entered your body when that person entered the room.

With that in mind, consider that there are two steps to ascertaining your own baseline:

- Make a list of what you perceive to be behaviors and vocal traits you have when you're relaxed.

- Ask someone else to follow the steps outlined previously, including differentiating between recall and imagining, to determine your baseline.

If you think the person trying to help you is off the mark when it comes to observing and listening, find someone else to do it.

Some people project far too much to be objective in this exercise. That is, they assume that a gesture that means something particular to them means the same to other people. Projection undermines the ability to see past one's own experiences and culture to determine what is "normal behavior." To whatever extent possible, we need to see and hear others without filtering our perceptions about their body language through our assumptions.

Is the baby orangutan in the photo sucking his thumb the way a human baby sucks a pacifier, sucking food off his thumb, or sucking his thumb because he hurt it? Is he teething and rubbing his gums? You don't know, because you do not have enough information. Whatever answer you give reflects projection—perhaps because you've seen a documentary about orangutans or maybe because he reminds you of your own child. Projection like this creeps into our observations of others so often that we don't even realize how powerfully it impacts our conclusions about the meaning of other people's actions. For purposes of clarity in this discussion, we will call projection that affects our perceptions *incoming projection.*

In the context of a body language discussion, projection has a companion meaning: conveying how you want another person to respond to you. We'll call this *outgoing projection.* You send messages you want other people to see and react to. This meaning of projection is integral to our guidance on proactively using body language as a sales tool so it comes into the conversation throughout the rest of the book.

In the next section, we help you organize your thoughts about what you observed and heard in your efforts to determine someone else's baseline.

Categories of Movement

Gregory Hartley (*The Art of Body Talk*) is a body language expert and the coauthor with Maryann of eight books on human behavior. He sorts most movements into four categories. We say "most" because some things people do fall outside of the primary categories; they show up because of culture, habit, health, or their relationship with another person. One example is a hand tremor associated with a neurological disease. Another might be a seated person absentmindedly swinging a leg that doesn't touch the ground. Another is *mirroring* behavior, which is associated with bonding with another person.

Hartley calls the main categories of movement the Big Four: illustrators, regulators, adaptors, and barriers.

Illustrators

Illustrators accentuate your message.

Examples include pointing an index finger when saying, "I mean it!" or shrugging shoulders when saying, "I don't know." Shifting your weight to signal impatience is an illustrator using the lower body.

When explaining the benefits of your services to a potential client, you might put both palms up to suggest "I'm giving you something."

Perhaps your baseline involves illustrators that are conservative—that is, arms close to the body and no high energy moves. You've deviated from baseline when you respond to a tough customer by throwing your arms in the air.

Illustrators could be unintentional or intentional, but it's helpful if you can spot the difference. In one case, they help you evaluate a person's typical behaviors and spot deviations from baseline; in the other, they alert you to the fact that the person rehearsed his presentation to the point that you aren't seeing a spontaneous or genuine response.

As people talk, they tend to automatically use their limbs to accent what they're saying. There is no deliberate choice associated with every move. In addition, however, some people learn illustrators when they study how to improve their presentations. They have a specific meaning they want to convey and choose illustrators very carefully. For example, they might be coached that extending a hand with the palm upward is an invitation, so they deliberately put it into their repertoire. Fundamentally, there's nothing wrong with that. Illustrators that are strong and fluid arouse a sense of belief in other people. Some people carry this to extremes, though, with their movements completely staged; that's when they can lose their intended impact or even work against the presenter.

Regulators

Regulators relate to conversation control.

Examples include nodding your head when you want someone to continue talking or putting your finger on your lips when you want the person to stop talking. A blatant regulator is turning and walking away while someone is talking. You may say something like, "Just off to the restroom. Back in a flash!" but the message is loud and clear: "I don't want to listen to any more of this at the moment."

You might want to stop your sales presentation and ask if your prospect has any questions if you see her pursing her lips. Without even realizing it, she may be telling you she's heard enough for now.

We don't usually think of regulators as an element of a baseline, but it's certainly possible that an individual would habitually do something that appears to be a regulator. For example, she may nod when another person is talking. That doesn't necessarily tell you much—unless the nodding suddenly stops.

The postures and movements associated with engaged listening encourage the other person to keep talking. In contrast, when you clamp your lips while someone is talking, you are sending the signal that you don't want to hear any more or you don't want to hear more of the same. When you turn away slightly, it's the same kind of indicator.

If you're trying to make a deadline or get to an appointment, there is a huge temptation to send signals that encourage people to curtail their explanations, avoid repetition, and leave your office or your meeting when they are done saying what they have to say. Just keep in mind that any overuse of regulators to get someone to abbreviate a conversation can damage your communication with another person. If at all possible, try not to stomp on someone's sentences. Listening is one of the most powerful tools you have to affect human behavior, so don't cut your listening short prematurely.

Adaptors

Adaptors are responses to anxiety.

Examples include rubbing an index finger and thumb together, playing with an earring, or clicking a pen. You are releasing nervous energy and/or doing something that you find soothing. When you watch professional sports, look for the quirky movements that they do before needing to perform: the pitcher rubbing his leg, the tennis player twirling her racket, the golfer tugging on his glove. These are all adaptors.

Your customer has just asked you how soon you can deliver the new product and you know it won't be for at least a month—and he needs it next week. You rub your neck before you give him the bad news.

Adaptors indicate stress is present so they are not part of a baseline. Some people have quirky moves that look like adaptors, but if someone habitually does something even when he's relaxed, then it's not an adaptor.

The use of adaptors is one of the clues of possible deception. Most people are not skilled at any level of deception, whether it's omitting a fact, distorting a fact, or embellishing a fact. Engaging in deception, even if it's minor, will probably cause some stress and that stress will leak out in the form of an adaptor.

On the positive side, you may see adaptors used by someone who finds you a little intimidating in a good way. You may be exceptionally intelligent, attractive, or well-dressed so the other person's use of adaptors is not a negative anxiety response, but actually a sign that he or she thinks you're pretty great.

Barriers

Barriers provide a shield from a perceived threat or are part of a power move to expand personal space.

Examples of shielding include turning away from someone or holding an object between you and a person you're talking with. An example of using a barrier as power move is sitting behind your large mahogany desk to conduct a meeting with a direct report.

A potential major donor to your art museum has reluctantly granted a meeting with you. You show up at his office and he's seated behind a large glass table, thereby establishing a lot of personal real estate and keeping you away.

A person's baseline could include very closed-in body language with arms typically held close the body and objects commonly held in front, effectively blocking close contact. Conversely, you may notice a person seems quite open, suggesting confidence and, perhaps, receptivity. These are unintentional movements that give you some insight into the comfort level of person when it comes to connecting through conversation and/or touch.

Barriers are potentially very useful. They can give you the distance and/or separation you require to feel comfortable, and they can also set you up as the person in charge. On the flip side, they can undermine your communication, intimidate people, and come across as downright rude. They can also make you look weak and afraid—as though you have to hide behind something in order to have a conversation.

Observing which seats people take in a conference room where there is no assigned seating can indicate the need for separation or the desire to establish importance. A prospect who selects a seat at the far end of the conference table is either trying to establish a long barrier to keep others away or to set himself up as the one who "owns" a lot of personal real estate, therefore, broadcast that he is the most important person in the room.

This example bridges into the concept of proxemics, which is complementary to barriers. It is the study of how much space we need in different situations—how proximity to another person or a group influences communication.

Let's say you're interacting with a customer with whom you have done business before and there is typically a high comfort level between you. You are pitching him on an upgrade to a product and notice that he seems to want to keep his distance. Maybe he even leaves the room briefly and when he returns, he sits in a chair that's a little further from the one he was in before. That is a distinct message that he is pulling away, reluctant or even resistant to letting you into his personal space. Maybe he doesn't believe the pitch. Maybe he wants to change vendors or products.

Now flip it. This is a customer you know well, have come to pitch him on an upgrade to a product, and he draws closer to you. Proximity conveys to you that he does not want or need distance from you or your message.

The concept of territoriality is also encompassed by this field of study. So even though you may be across the room from your customer, when you sit in his favorite conference room chair, you may get the same kind of response as if you leaned forward and invaded his personal space.

To recap:

Category	Definition
Illustrator	A movement that accentuates your message; could be any part of the body, but most often we think in terms of arm and hand movement.
Regulator	Something you do to control the conversation: curtail it, encourage it, speed it up, or slow it down.
Adaptor	A response to anxiety that puts nervous energy into a particular place and makes you feel better, such as a rubbing or petting gesture.
Barrier	A shield from a perceived threat, regardless of how minor, or a power move to expand personal real estate.

Commonalities in Movement

If determining baseline is the most fundamental skill in understanding and using body language, then the next level up is interpreting movements that humans have in common. We sort them into two categories: ***universal human movements*** and ***common cultural movements.***

Universal Human Movements

As a species, we have very few movements and vocal expressions in common. One of them is universal facial expressions that capture the following eight emotions:

1. Fear.

2. Anger.

3. Surprise.

4. Disgust.

5. Sadness.

6. Contempt.

7. Happiness.

8. Pride.

We want to point out that none of the emotions is inherently bad; there is a time and place when all of them are appropriate. At the same time, the first six are often undesirable in the context of a sales encounter. As we explore in Chapter 3, seeing them on the face of a prospect or customer could signal trouble for you.

Psychologist Paul Ekman discovered that humans around the world use the same muscles when expressing these eight emotions with the face. He went through an exhaustive process interviewing people in different countries and different cultures; it was the foundation for a lifetime of extraordinary discovery regarding the expression of human emotion.[1]

There are a few other involuntary facial expressions that express recognition of another person or idea, skepticism, and confusion. These are not emotions—not like the responses that Ekman studied—but rather cognitive processes that manifest in identifiable ways in the face. Just think how well you will be served by the ability to recognize these actions and expressions in a sales setting!

When he served as a wartime military interrogator, Greg Hartley saw that prisoners who denied knowing each other when in separate rooms would display a momentary eyebrow flash when brought together. It's just a quick raise of the brows rather than the kind of prolonged brow lift you would see when someone is surprised. He observed time and again that this eyebrow flash was a sure sign that the prisoners recognized each other. The same kind of facial movement would occur when you see someone walking toward you on the street, for example, and you think it might be someone you know. If you hear a concept that rings true for you, you are likely to do it as well. When you detect this sign of affirmation during a sales encounter, it can serve you well; you've hit a chord.

The lack of it can signal an opposite response. That is, you throw out a concept you think the other person should respond to with familiarity and get nothing—a blank look. That would mean it's time to reconsider how well the person is relating to your presentation, product, or service. Maybe your set-up is lacking.

"Request for approval" (an expression called "outer brow raiser" in Ekman nomenclature) is another Hartley concept that is easy to confirm. Watch politicians at press conferences: They hear a question that pushes them a little off balance. They give an answer they hope is on target for the audience. Hope that the answer is on target—as opposed to certainty that it is on target—affects the person's facial expression. The facial muscles arch the brows, and the mouth may look a bit drawn or there may be a tight-lipped smile. It is the look of someone expressing "You believe me, don't you?"

Your request-for-approval expression would generally be involuntary. If your prospect or customer sees it in the context of a sales encounter, even without familiarity of the concept, that individual would detect uncertainty. On some level, she would pick up your hope that you hit the right note as opposed to the certainty that you did. As an aside, it is possible to use this expression as a trigger to get your prospect to ask questions or contribute to the discussion.

Another couple of movements we could call universal are eye movements associated with cognitive thought and problem-solving, which are functions that occur in the frontal lobe. When you are analyzing or calculating, you might move your eyes down and to left. In fact, you may even move your whole head in that direction. Movement of eyes or the head down and to the right suggests intense feelings. If you watch the heads of people at funeral or other event where strong emotions are affecting people, you will see this occurring.

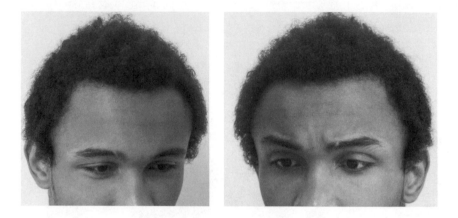

Commonality in Culture

Any group that shares beliefs and customs could be described as having its own culture—a gang, a religious organization, a nation, a family. Cultural norms often can be categorized in terms of the Big Four and the energy associated with them. Think of the stereotypical representation of a Latin or Italian man or woman "talking with the hands," or the conservative illustrators that once exemplified the movements of people from many Asian cultures. Gestures common to a culture, however, can also include movements that have nothing to do with the Big Four. They help differentiate the people in one culture from members of another, with some examples being those associated with people who share a religion or are part of the same street gang.

In the United States, people commonly associate crossing arms with uncertainty and the need for distance; it is seen as a barrier, whether it meant to be or not.

Knit brows, such as those captured in the image on this page, tend to signal confusion or uncertainty. This is also a part of the world where sustained eye contact evokes the perception of honesty and confidence, whereas some other cultures consider it rude. Use of the middle finger has a specific insulting meaning throughout the United States, but it translates well in multiple languages and cultures. And although people in the United States see thumbs up as an affirmative gesture, it's considered extremely foul in many other cultures.

It is always important to consider the culture of the people in baselining as well as interpreting the meaning of a person's movements. With an ever-increasing need to establish sales relationships with people from around the world, it's vital to have sensitivity to the impact of culture on body language.

Learning to Read

Although body type, culture, and context will affect movements people choose to convey certain meanings, it is possible to make some generalities about what constitutes open or closed body language.

Open body language is actions and facial expressions that are invitational; they show a desire to connect and suggest that trust is present. The body language of happiness and many other positive mental states and emotions will contain movements suggesting openness.

Closed body language projects the desire to shield and separate; it neither inspires trust nor suggests receptivity to building it. The body language of disgust, contempt, or other negative mental states and emotions will contain closed movements.

In baselining someone, if the individual really is in a relatively relaxed state, you're more likely to see openness. However, some people create comfort through barriers and habitual movements that look like adaptors. In other words, you might see a little of each style in a person's baseline.

Examples of open body language are:

- A smile with the eyes engaged. That means you'll see some wrinkles around the eyes unless the person suffers from a neurological disorder or has had Botox injections to temporarily paralyze certain facial muscles so that wrinkles don't appear.

- Illustrators that include open palms and arms comfortably away from the body rather than shielding it.

- Regulators such as head nods and attentive eye contact that encourage continued conversation.

- Minimal or no reliance on adaptors; a sense of calm in conversation.

- Minimal or no barriers. There is a good comfort level with the other person, a sense of easy interaction that makes barriers unnecessary.

Examples of closed body language are the opposite:

- A fake smile. Only the mouth and muscles around it are moving.

- Illustrators that might include clenched hands or hands that suggest pushing the other person away. Arm movements could be either close to the body—and here, we are bridging over to what might also be a barrier—or aggressive. Flailing or whipping movements can be ways of repelling another person. Legs can also be part of closed body language. Some people will cross their legs because it feels like a protective position; others do it out of habit or comfort.

- Regulators such as head shakes and avoidance of eye contact discourage continued conversation.

- Use of adaptors because some degree of nervousness is present gives a sense that a trusting connection is absent, at least at the moment.

- The need for barriers—increasing the size of one's personal real estate and reinforcing shielding from another person—typifies closed body language.

Vocal Characteristics

Listening and watching for changes in vocal expression is one way of determining how relaxed or strained a person is. *Vocalics* is an area of non-verbal communication studies because it's about how something is said rather than what is being said. There are three facets of vocalics that often indicate emotion and always tell you something about how to interpret what's being said to you: vocal qualities, emphasis, and use of fillers.

Vocal Qualities

Pitch, tone, pace, volume, hoarseness, stridency, and nasality are among the characteristics of a voice. In some cases, they can change from moment to moment, reflecting a deviation from the speaker's baseline.

Pitch

Pitch helps convey the intensity of the communication, express a question, or convey uncertainty or even deception. A woman's who's just been crowned Miss Universe will likely say, "Thank you! Thank you!" in a high-pitched voice. And typically, a person's voice will rise at the end of a question (although there are cultures where the opposite is true), so "How long does it take to get from here to Nashville?" would have the pitch rise on the word "Nashville."

Regarding the expression of uncertainty or untruth, there is often a rise in pitch suggesting that the next thing you should do is agree with him. For example, at the end of a sales presentation before the "ask," a sales rep might say, "The product is much more reliable than what you are currently using" with the pitch rising on the word "using." If this is accompanied by the request-for-approval facial expression, then the change in pitch is an important nonverbal signal. It is working in tandem with a facial movement that involves slightly raised eyebrows to suggest "You believe me, don't you?" or "I have a concern that you don't believe me."

Tone (word some w/ the stroke or whatever (two))

Tone is a characteristic of voice that goes a long way toward conveying meaning. Much of what we learned about tone, we may have learned from our parents when we were small children. Mom asks the child to do something he has no interest in doing and the child says, "Yes, Mommy" in a way that provokes "Don't you use that tone of voice with me, young man!"

Tone and pitch work in tandem to convey sarcasm, to clue you in that someone is telling a joke, to leak repressed anger, and much more. They lend nuance to speech to help clarify a message and the intent of the message.

Pace

Pace is the speaking rate someone has adopted in a particular conversation. A sudden change is a deviation from baseline in the context of that conversation and it indicates stress. On a business call earlier this year, Jim detected that the person he was speaking with had quickened the pace of his speech. He looked at the time and realized that it was about three minutes before eleven o'clock. Even though there was no established time to end the call and they still had ground to cover, Jim said, "Do you have another appointment at 11?" The client said yes and expressed surprise at the perceptive question.

A person who is not being completely honest might either speed up or slow down. Speeding up is one way someone who is trying to deceive you can prevent you from interrupting him with a question or challenge. And if the person suddenly changes the pace by enunciating every word, in contrast to fluid speech that preceded the shift, you have reason to question the veracity of the statement.

Volume

Volume is another vocal quality that conveys intensity. An ardent denial of an accusation would probably be said more loudly than other parts of the conversation. Of course, some people might drop to a whisper in expressing a denial as if they are embarrassed at their attempt at a cover-up. Neither change would automatically suggest that the person is being deceitful, though. You would need to analyze the person's movements to see if they reinforce your suspicions, as well as to ask questions that get the person to revisit the information or retell the story. Questioning techniques to accomplish this are covered in Chapter 4.

Stridency/Hoarseness

Qualities such as stridency or hoarseness suggest stress only when they are not normal for the person. When the vocal chords tighten up and/or the throat becomes dry, the voice takes on a different sound. It can get very raspy, but for some people, that coarseness is part of their baseline. Look for other signs of stress, like an increase in blink rate. If the throat is drying out due to a mild fight-or-flight response, then the eyes are drying out, too, and the person will automatically blink more often. You might also see the person's body get more rigid if the vocal chords are tightening.

•••••••••

When you consider how much meaning and emotion can be conveyed by pitch, tone, pace, volume, and stridency, it's easy to see why people often rely on emojis and emoticons in texts and emails. A purist would probably argue that selecting the right words would avert any misunderstanding about attitude or intent, but we all know how flawed an assumption that is. You might text a colleague after a meeting, "The sales call lasted three hours!" Maybe to her, a long meeting is her worst nightmare, but what you mean to suggest is that you and prospect hit it off so well that the meeting ended up being long. Putting a "thumbs up" after the text is a decent substitute for a shift in vocal quality that suggests excitement. (Some people would probably benefit by inserting emojis into their face-to-face conversations, too.)

Emphasis

Emphasis can be expressed in multiple ways. One syllable or word may have more volume behind it, or there may be a noticeable change in pitch from one word to the next. Another way to emphasize would be to "isolate" a word by pausing before and after it, as in, "How...dare...you accuse me of showing the report to her?" You could also stretch out a word or sound: "Nooooo, that is not a problem we have ever had with this software." A really annoying use of emphasis is simply repeating words or even whole statements over and over again.

Deliberate use of emphasis is a vocal illustrator when you are accentuating your message by using it—and you probably will reinforce the emphasis through your body language. You are spotlighting your intent to gain the full attention of your listener on the message you are currently conveying.

There is an opposite reason to use emphasis, however, and that is to obscure a point. Emphasizing one word over the others around it puts attention on one part of the sentence over the others: "After reading the report, I had a huge sense of *relief* despite the fact that the company made less money than we'd hoped for in that quarter."

Emphasizing certain syllables or words can alter the entire meaning of a sentence as well.

Let's play around with this Howard Hughes (Leonardo DiCaprio) line from the movie *The Aviator*:

Don't tell me it can't be done!	You are warned not to saying anything.
Don't **tell** me it can't be done!	You could write it down, maybe.
Don't tell **me** it can't be done!	Go ahead and tell someone else; just don't say it to me.
Don't tell me **it** can't be done!	You can tell me other things can't be done, but not "it."
Don't tell me it **can't** be done!	Just tell me it can be done.

A final reason to use emphasis is to show how excited you are. In that case, you might hit hard on every word in a sentence, just to exhibit your passion for the message. Even a body-language rookie would spot that as a major deviation from baseline. This would also be an annoying way to communicate passion.

Use of Fillers

Typical fillers in English are "um," "uh," "well," "like," and "you know," but it's important to note that fillers are not a distinctly

English language phenomenon. You will find them creeping into conversation in many languages. American Sign Language even contains gestures for fillers. Use of fillers is part of the baseline for some people. A lot of young people use the word *like* constantly. It's an annoying generational thing that has become ubiquitous.

Many of us who are trained to avoid fillers may succeed in not using ums and ahs, but we still find ourselves using a silent filler, otherwise known as a pause. The main thing to note is that, if it's not part of the person's baseline, then it may be time to probe into why there is hesitation in a response.

Appearance and Props

Your first look at a prospect can give you insights about your conversation might go. If you see precision in the way the person dresses, then the person is likely to value a high degree of control and predictability in his life. If you have the opportunity to meet in the person's office and it, too, reflects precision and organization, you have confirmation that a certain amount of rigidity is comfortable for the individual. These features are all part of the individual's baseline behavior. Someone like that might be expressing strong emotion by crumpling a piece of paper and leaving it on the conference table, whereas that action might have very little meaning for someone who has a casual, disorganized office.

You also convey important information about yourself in your appearance, including your choice of clothing, your posture, and the props you carry. Every time you get dressed for a sales meeting, ask yourself what qualities you want to project. Precision and discipline? Creativity and enthusiasm? Alertness and authority? Your appearance needs to reinforce what you are doing with your body and voice to connect with a client, build rapport, and establish trust.

Summary Points

- Determining an individual's baseline is the fundamental skill of reading and using body language.

- Make sure you know the characteristics of your own baseline as well as that of your prospects and customers.

- Incoming projection is a filter created by one's own experiences and culture; it undermines your ability to read someone's body language.

- In the context of this body language discussion, projection has a companion meaning: conveying how you want another person to respond to you. We call it outgoing projection.

- Four important categories of movement are illustrators, regulators, barriers, and adaptors.

- Human beings have a few commonalities in movement, particularly the facial expressions for fear, anger, happiness, surprise, disgust, sadness, contempt, and pride.

- It is possible to make some generalities about body language that is considered "open" (invitational) and "closed" (shielding).

- Certain vocal characteristics are part of non-verbal communication because they are more about how something is said rather than what is said.

- Appearance and props are part of a person's body language, giving clues about an individual's behavior.

3

....

ELEMENTS OF A
SALES RELATIONSHIP

Five factors characterize a sales encounter: connection, curiosity, deference, preference, and desire. Here are our definitions and importance of each concept in sales:

- **Connection** means a good relationship of any duration. It builds in stages with those stages occurring in a single meeting or over time. Your body language should reinforce the growing sense of trust between you and the prospect.

- **Curiosity** means genuine interest, both in the person you are meeting with and in that person's ideas. Curiosity maintains the vitality of the connection—and it needs to be mutual. The active listening you used to help establish a connection plays a key role, signaling that you want to know what the prospect or client is telling you. In turn, questions from the person about your company and your product or service should indicate that the curiosity is reciprocated.

- **Deference** means regard and respect. It has the connotation of putting someone above you, perhaps just momentarily. The placement of deference generally shifts back and forth in a sales relationship with the body language similarly going from the projection of control and authority to recognizing the control and authority of the other person. The pendulum swing typically does something like this: (1) You display and express deference related to your appreciation at having a meeting with the person. (2) The prospect or client shows you deference as you describe the quality of your product and power of your solution to her problem. (3) You return to a more deferential posture in acknowledging the decision authority of the person.

- **Preference** means fondness and predilection. It could be an overt or a subliminal influence, so subtle that the person has no idea it exists as a key factor in decision-making. For some, it could be the preference to be in the company of an attractive or pleasant individual, as opposed to someone who is neither. A preference could also mean the person is predisposed to favor domestic products over imports, or the other way around. In the course of a sales encounter, prospects might reveal that a preference exists by changes in body language; they exude feelings that they might not even be aware of.

- **Desire** is a longing, a need. It makes the close possible when the desire is for a solution, resolution, fulfillment, engagement, or other factor that improves the person's business circumstances. The sense that a need is being fulfilled should grow stronger throughout the encounter until the inevitable occurs: the sale is made.

The "body language of rapport-building" is how we will describe the set of actions that help build connection. We will also look at some of the specific things you might do to express and arouse curiosity, show deference and accept that it is being shown to you, and recognize the indicators of desire. We will also guide you in what body language can help you determine the preferences of people in your meeting.

Connection

Sales professionals need to establish trust, collect accurate information, and leave prospects and customers with a lingering good feeling about them. The foundation for success in all three areas is forging a positive connection. For some people, the ability to do this comes naturally; for others, it's a learned skill. They have to study it like an engineer has to study calculus. In an interview focused on rapport-building, Elizabeth Bancroft, executive director of the Association of Former Intelligence Officers, expressed this sentiment: "There are traits—some ethnic, perhaps, and some the result of upbringing—that predispose certain people to be gifted at connecting with others and eliciting information. For the same reasons, other people have no gift for these things and it would be harder for them to cultivate rapport-building skills."[1]

Here is a list of rapport-building techniques that will help you either freshen your skills or start from scratch in developing them. The how-to for each of the 10 techniques is explored in some detail following the list:

1. Smile with your eyes.

2. Use touch carefully.

3. Share something with the person about yourself.

4. Mirror the other person.

5. Treat everyone with respect.

6. Reinforce trust through open body language.

7. Suspend your ego.

8. Flatter and praise.

9. Take your time in listening.

10. Get your prospect talking *and* moving.

Smile With Your Eyes

It's the look you give to someone you are genuinely happy to see. In this case, a picture is worth a thousand words.

Use Touch Carefully

We are not talking about revitalizing the campaign in which people carry or wear a sign offering "free hugs." We are talking about using the science of **haptic communication** to your advantage.

Haptics is the study of communication by touch, with haptic communication referring specifically to nonverbal communication that refers to the ways in which people and animals interact meaningfully via the sense of touch. (The science has expanded to include haptic technologies, but we are using the term in a more classic sense.) Researchers in this field have found hard evidence that touch improves interaction in a variety of situations. For example, students evaluated a library and its staff more favorably if the librarian briefly touched the patron while returning his or her library card, female restaurant servers received larger tips when they touched patrons, and people were more likely to sign a petition when the petitioner touched them during their interaction.

We offer this insight with a caveat. In a sales situation, it is possible to progress from a handshake to other, minimal touch, depending on the circumstances and the level of rapport that's developing. Touch can serve as a physical reminder of the connection that's forming. But "touch" can be interpreted broadly, as the following image suggests. In it, the consultant and his client are simply touching the same device. In our definition of the term, this could also be considered haptic communication. Similar proximity might involve jointly working through a problem on a whiteboard or just handing the person a cup of coffee as opposed to letting him pour it himself,

Note that your touch communication with a business contact is shaped by your knowledge of the person's culture, including the corporate culture, and facts about the person's demeanor that you picked up during baselining.

Share Something About Yourself With the Person

There is a huge difference between "getting personal" and revealing selected facts about yourself. A prospect should not have to hear about your nasty divorce, but may feel a connection with you by knowing where you went to college or your recreational pursuits. Your homework on the individual you're meeting with should give you at least a handful of facts about education, work history, non-work interests, and so on, that give you ways to introduce related facts about yourself. A quick web search yields a lot.

The payoff for your efforts is an effective incentive to promote conversation aimed at connecting. Think about how this works on a date (or think back to how this worked on a date if you've been out of that scene for a while). Your date says, "Sorry about the interruption. That call was from my mom." You say, "Where does your mom live?" She says, "Philadelphia." You say, "I went to school at UPenn!" Suddenly, you are visualizing the same streets and sharing memories that you can both relate to, even though they don't reflect shared experiences.

Mirror the Other Person

People like people who seem similar to them in presentation and conversation. Be cautious, though, because you do not want to mimic the other person; that will instantly destroy rapport.

Mirroring is generally subtle, whether you do it with your voice or your body, and it's often automatic. In fact, it's so natural that you might surprise yourself at how easily and often you do it. Four common ways that we mirror other people are:

- **Choice of word or phrase.** Industries, companies, departments, and teams may all have a working vocabulary specific to their needs, mission, and objectives. Using selected words or phrases that suggest you have paid attention and absorbed keywords supports connection. Using a caliber of vocabulary that matches that of your contact is another form of mirroring; if he tends to be monosyllabic, don't go reaching for the mile-long academic words. On a more automatic level, if a person uses a phrase that "sounds right" to you, you might start using it without thinking.

- **Pacing.** It might be the cadence associated with regional speech or a pace reflecting personal style. When you find yourself talking at the same rate as the other person, it is not acting or "faking it." It's mirroring that comes naturally to people who want to connect with another person.

- ~~Energy level.~~ ~~You want to be in roughly the same arena as the person you are trying to connect with.~~ ~~Overwhelm~~ing ~~an even-keeled or low-energy person with your volume and pace or with~~ movements that are highly energetic will push that person away. Just wait for the barriers to show up! In contrast, if your meeting is with a person ~~who tends to scurry around and talk fast and~~ you are ~~extremely reserved, you have a mismatch that~~ can cause ~~d~~istance rather than support connection.

- **Movement.** ~~Mirroring could be a slight lean in the same direction as the other person or using an arm position that's simila~~r. Yawning in response to another person's yawn is involuntary mirroring. Deliberate mirroring to enhance a developing rapport means getting the gist of the other person's movements rather than duplicating them. ~~In this image, the two people meeting are barrier-ing in a similar manner, squaring their shoulders in a similar manner, and maintaining eye contact.~~ A salient point is that each ~~person has gender-specific ways of adopting the same posture.~~ The following image demonstrates a successful example of mirroring.

Treat Everyone With Respect

Suppose you're a 50-ish sales professional wearing a jacket and slacks making a presentation to a 28-year-old internet security specialist with sleeve tattoos and blue-streaked hair. If you expect to be treated with respect by others, then that's how you have to treat them. Body language and tone of voice that suggest anything but respect will be detected, if only subliminally. You may have to remind yourself that ink on the arm does not alter a person's intelligence or personality as you look for ways to connect in a genuine way.

Over the course of years of interviews, we have heard what some people would consider horror stories about this challenge. In these scenarios, the person who needed to connect with another person felt as though his or her values were being assaulted in showing respect. Lena Sisco, a decorated interrogator and founder of the Congruency Group, noted in Maryann's book *Nothing but the Truth* that there was a particular emotional challenge of establishing rapport with members of the Taliban who had done horrific things to people. Yet her job as a military interrogator depended on the ability to connect with them with respect; she had to remind herself, "At the end of the day, they are still human beings. To get them to talk to me, they have to feel honest respect from me."[2]

Among the simpler, more common ways to show respect for another person are to silence your mobile phone before a meeting and not interrupt the person while she's talking.

Reinforce Trust Through Open Body Language

Open body language is invitational: no barriers between you and the other person, including crossed arms and laptop computers; eye contact that shows you are genuinely attentive; and a

~relaxed demeanor that puts another person at ease and makes it easy to sit in the same room with you.

The opposite is body language that shields key vulnerable areas, namely, the nape of the neck, torso, and area just below the waist. In this context, we don't want to think of them as areas of vulnerability, however. When you expose them with confidence you inspire trust, and in the context of sales, they are better termed "power zones."

For simplicity, we will call these three areas the neck, navel, and groin. With that in mind, here are examples of the *opposite* of what you aim for.

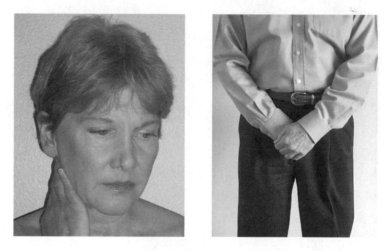

As you look at these examples of ways to block the power zones, consider how commonly you might use such barriers with no intention of shutting out another person. Barriers like those depicted convey a definite sense that you either feel ill-at-ease or distanced from the other person in the room—not perceptions that support rapport-building.

Suspend Your Ego

In general, people like to exhibit their expertise and experience. It makes them feel smart and worthwhile. Show interest when the person you're meeting with tries to tell you how to do something or explains a concept to you. Let her educate you.

The ability to suspend your ego makes you more likeable and the other person more open to your requests and input. In other words, ego suspension helps create a path of less resistance. Remember that ego suspension means that the exchange is principally about the other person. Be attentive without faking it. False interest is easy to read.

Now for the hard part. By definition, ego is inextricably linked with who you are and what you're worth. If you're making a solution sale or an expertise sale, for example, then you have to be perceived as the best person to address the customer's problem and/or to advise him on a crucial business matter. But do not underestimate the power of humility in gaining someone's trust. There is nothing wrong with appreciating your self-worth and letting your professional value and knowledge shine through in conversation, but there is a lot wrong with putting them center stage and throwing a spotlight on them.

If you can master the ability to make your prospect or customer feel respected for his competence and knowledge, you have gone a long way toward convincing her that you are a worthy and able partner.

Flatter and Praise

Genuine compliments energize people. They help lift a person up and make him feel as though you appreciate what he has to offer in the meeting. It's not a matter of buttering up the person, as much as it is voicing the fact that you notice something worth noticing.

Your positive remarks do not need to be an observation about the person you're meeting with. They can be about the organization, facility, culture, the trophies in the lobby, or fact that there is a parking space outside for the deceased founder of the company. Jim actually saw this and was moved at the caring culture of the organization. Employees had decided to permanently set aside a parking space for the man who made their careers possible.

If you not only notice something like that, but also show that you care about it, then you connect in a persuasive way.

Take Your Time in Listening

In the upcoming section on curiosity, we explore the skill of active listening in depth. This is a critical skill that will serve you well both professionally and personally. The summary point to remember is that the best listening is done with your whole body. When someone thinks that you have drifted away from the conversation, perhaps because you've turned away, are shuffling in your seat, or glancing at your phone, you have reduced rapport.

As part of your vigorous listening, pay attention to any unique vocabulary the person uses. Adopting keywords shows you are paying attention. For example, if you client talks about not "having eyes on the problem," that's a phrase that has meaning for him. Make a mental note of it and, when appropriate, use it when you talk about the solution you're offering him. Don't wait for the meeting to pick up keywords and phrases, either. Make sure your homework on the industry and the company includes nomenclature used in the space. You should walk in with a handle on buzzwords that relate to operations, mission, and other aspects of the business.

Get Your Prospect Talking *and* Moving

When you ask yes-or-no question, some people actually give a *yes* or *no* in response—and nothing more. Ask questions that require a narrative response. These are questions that begin with an interrogative—that is, who, what, when, where, how, and why.

As a complement to talking, when you move the conversation from one physical location to another, you have set the stage for taking your rapport-building to the next level. In discussing a major donation to an art museum, for example, you could take your prospect into the framing shop to get a behind-the-scenes look at a relatively unique expertise that is vital to your operation. If you are visiting your customer's facility, always accept the invitation to tour it, even if you're toured it before. Be attentive; look for changes that may have been made and comment on them as part of showing your interest. Once a person has experienced a connection with you in different environments, the bond between you strengthens.

••••••••••

Even if you are adept at these positive rapport-building techniques, some people resist a connection to another person. It doesn't matter that this may be something they actually want; they still push back. Here are some reasons why you and your prospect may have some barriers to forging a connection:

- The person does not perceive that you share a value system. Maybe because of something you said, or wore, or something that was said about you, the individual feels distanced from you. For example, let's say it's July 3rd and you are in a "heartland" region of the United States where patriotism is openly exhibited. You are meeting with a CEO that your homework indicates is active in local politics. Although you have a suit on that's accompanied by your warmest smile, you are not wearing a label pin with the Stars and Stripes on it—suggesting that perhaps you are not keenly aware that the following day is July 4th, America's Independence Day. Whether the CEO's response to you comes from observation and judgment, or from a subliminal reaction to the lack of a flag symbol, you just lost ground in your efforts to build rapport.

- Your customer or prospect feels as though you do not have a positive relationship with her team or trusted advisors. If you have done anything to alienate a gatekeeper or influencer in her life, you will likely be held at a distance.

- Negative emotions dominate. How would you act with the principal of the company you are meeting with if you were kept waiting for 45 minutes in a windowless conference room without even being offered water? If your frustration surfaces in the first moments of a meeting with that person, you can probably forget about building a rapport with him.

- You come across as disingenuous. You may just be distracted because of a fender bender on your way to the meeting, or perhaps you do not feel well so your focus is off and your energy level is low. Regardless of the reason, if you prospect does not perceive you as fully present and engaged, you could be perceived as insincere. This is a time when your knowledge of body language can help you move past a major problem quickly.

Before trying to establish rapport with someone, consider if there might be such circumstantial, ideological, or other barriers that will complicate your task.

Another barrier to developing strong positive rapport is a sense of threat. Later in the book, we explore a sales approach we call fear selling that involves a measure of intimidation, the suggestion being that the customer stands to lose a lot—money, brand recognition, proprietary data, or something else—unless he hires you or buys your product. In most situations, instilling fear on any level works against you because fear is such a powerful emotion. When it surfaces, a person's body experiences automatic changes in blood flow and muscle tension; these make it hard for the person to calm down and have a rational conversation. When there is the presence of a threat—a threat you can theoretically alleviate—a connection might be made, but without a lot of positive feelings. A bond shaped by intimidation may be effective in the short run, but it is not an effective long-term strategy.

Curiosity

Curiosity is a science, not "just" an intellectual response to something we find interesting. The Center for Curiosity in New York promotes research initiatives on the subject and currently has projects underway at the University of Pennsylvania in Philadelphia and Indian Institute of Technology Gandhinagar in India. The importance of this to you is that a segment of the research the Center is spearheading concerns the importance of curiosity in business, most notably consumer behavior and the impact of curiosity on workplace performance. Curiosity is a seriously important element in our business relationships.

Curiosity results from our natural inclination as people to be stimulus-seeking. As a sales professional, if you can enhance it by asking a question or providing information that lights a fire under a person's interest, you have moved your rapport-building efforts to a new level.

Curiosity strengthens the connection that is forming between you and your prospect. Two big ways to do this are through the quality of information you offer, and the associated presentation of it, and through your active listening.

Be Provocative

A June 2011 article for *Forbes* offered "5 Tips for Presenting Boring Technical Information—so It Isn't Boring."[3] The tips offered by *Forbes* contributor Nick Morgan merit focus because they help steer anyone toward arousing curiosity in people through the content and style in which information is presented. In going through those five recommendations—substantially paraphrased here to focus on sales—we also create a set-up to highlight the body language associated with being provocative.

- Presenting information is about persuasion, not only information. Yes, you will be telling the prospect or client about key features of your offering. At the same time, you are persuading the person those features are actually *key*—that is, the reason they are worth talking about is that they have value.

- Tying your information to solving a well-defined problem. Describe the problem and the pain it causes for the person. Follow that with an honest statement of how you can help solve it.

- Using stories and case studies to give life to your ability to solve problems. This is not to say that numbers should be ignored—"You can save $100,000 a year by doing this"— but rather that a story about a company saving $100,000 a year anchors the value of what you have to offer.

- Weaving metaphors and analogies into your presentation. If your database software has an ability to prevent hacking that endangers proprietary information, then you could say, "It's like a vaccine."

- Inviting your audience to give the answers to the questions that keep the presentation moving. Ask the people in the meeting, "How would *you* solve this if you had unlimited resources?" or "What does a successful public relations campaign look like to your CEO?"

With all of these tips, your ability to boost curiosity relates to how much you show interest in the audience's reactions and affirmation of their responses. It's great that they "get" what you have to say, but their engagement goes to a new level if they feel their responses have provoked new thoughts in you. In short, being provocative is ideally a reciprocal experience in which the audience gets the sense they are being provocative with you, too.

Use Active Listening

Active listening is one of the most critical tools you can have in trying to reinforce the rapport you're trying to build with someone. It's a magical way of getting people to share information.

Active listening has physical, intellectual, and emotional components.

Intellectual

You listen for keywords, which might be indicated by emphasis or how frequently they are used. Sometimes the keywords give you an obvious message. Someone who makes frequent references to taking a break or getting away for a while might actually be quite focused on finding vacation time.

You also want to listen for words that aren't there, but you would expect them to be there. For example, if the point of your meeting is to discuss computer-related security needs and the customer never even says the word *security,* the omission tells you he is avoiding the topic on some level. Similarly, someone who got a bad performance review and talks about everything except the performance review is probably broadcasting a message that she's upset about the performance review.

Let's look at that latter scenario—omission of keywords. Here three examples of the significance of this that Jim that noted while doing executive coaching. These were with three senior executives named Bill, Josh, and Darrow. Bill is in finance, Josh is in technology, and Darrow owns a couple of electrical contracting companies.

1. For a couple of sessions, Bill harped on the shortcomings of one of his staff members. The person seemed to be going in circles. He wasn't delivering. Jim helped Bill uncover the real issue, which is that Bill felt that he wasn't asserting leadership. Until that point, Bill had skirted the subject of his leadership role and responsibilities with the failing staff member.

2. In a related example, Josh talked endlessly about systems. Putting time-management systems in place. Making inventory systems run smoothly. Again, the issue wasn't technical: It wasn't about having systems that helped the company stay on track. Josh's real concern was the lack of personal accountability in the company. He avoided addressing that directly by focusing on systems.

3. With Darrow, he expressed concerns about strategic planning. Over and over, he talked about the imperative to implement a new planning process. The core issue here, which he kept side-stepping, was access to capital. He was uncomfortable talking about what he needed to do to get an infusion of cash, so he shifted his conversations to a related activity.

Physical

What you do and what you don't do with your body, including your voice, can signal the other person that you are listening carefully. Your posture, gestures, focus, energy, tone of voice, pace of speech, and word choices can either reassure someone that you're listening and not judging, or shut the other person down. These are all types of regulators.

Invitational body language involves looking at the person you're talking with. If you ask someone a question and then put your eyes on your computer, that's not the body language of active listening.

Your vocal patterns should be whatever is normal for you when you're not under stress. In other words, if a customer is telling you something that is emotionally charged, if you want to use active listening to encourage her to tell you the whole story, then try to keep your tone of voice and pace of speech as even as possible. It's in these tough conversational moments that active listening is an invaluable tool to communicate stability and engender trust.

Emotional

Listening to a client share feelings with you is likely to arouse some kind of emotional response. And if it doesn't, or you find yourself annoyed, we recommend hiding those facts.

Even though you want your tone and pace to be normal while you're listening, at some point, it can help to show how you feel, too. In a business setting, there's a kind of *quid pro quo* with this—that is, the exchange of "something for something" or "this for that." We'll get into the mechanics of *quid pro quo* as a questioning tactic later, but the key thing to remember here is that you aren't out to top the other person in terms of emotion, but just to let a little leak so the person feels like you're really connecting.

You're regulating the conversation through your active listening techniques.

Deference

The dance associated with deference involves alternating who is leading. The reciprocal nature of the exchange lends a balance and flow to a sales encounter. It is part of human nature to want to have a give-and-take relationship with others, so when deference is one-sided, the conversation seems awkward. And for the party who never feels deference, she might also experience resentment at not being shown respect; it's as though her ideas and opinions have no value to you.

Because of the reciprocity inherent in the shift of esteem from one person to another, deference helps create the ideal environment for persuasion, "the art of getting people to do things that are in their own best interest that also benefit you."[4] By showing regard for the other person's input, you make it clear that you are not making assumptions about what she needs, wants, or expects. You make it easier to persuade her to say *yes* to your product or service. When the time is right and you've collected the information you need, then you can move into the spotlight.

When it's your turn to take the lead, you need the body language of a confident person. You want to maintain comfortable eye contact, stand or sit up straight, and use illustrators that invite the person to "take" your information, as the following photo suggests. Mirroring is also important here because you want to reinforce the connection you are forging, even though it's your turn to shine.

Body language that suggests you do not feel as though you are in control—that you don't deserve deference—includes these tells:

- A higher-than-normal blink rate. A normal blink rate would be about six to eight times a minute, with the rate increasing if the eyes are a bit dry. What would cause that? Stress.

- The use of adaptors. As soon as you rub your neck, chew on your lips, play with your earring, or show any other actions that suggest anxiety, you weaken your position in the room.

- Holding your elbows close to your ribs. This suggests you need protection—that you are not comfortable at the moment.

- Knitting your brows. This is a look that might be simply that you're paying attention—it's the way you show interest—but most people would look at that facial movement and wonder, "What's wrong?"

- Pursing your lips. ~~Depending on how you do it, you will either look upset or like you're holding something back.~~

Preference

Determining a customer's preference in the context of this discussion has nothing to do with advanced analytics software. That kind of technology is useful for companies emailing offers after collecting data based on online activity, but ~~we're talking about reading a customer's body language to find out more about what he wants~~. More specifically, you want to read him to ascertain ~~what product~~ or ~~service *you*~~ have that appeals to him most.

Let's start with the premise that preferences aren't necessarily rational. The skin of many oranges, especially those from warm countries, is green. Consumers want oranges to be the color orange, though, so producers expose them to ethylene gas, or scrub them and dip them in dye. We have an irrational preference for orange oranges.

Building on the irrationality theme, we know that research conducted by Yale University psychologists looked at why many people "resist acquiring scientific information that clashes with common-sense intuitions about the physical and psychological domains."[5] In other words, their preference is to disregard documented facts and believe what feels right to them. If you are trying to focus a prospect's or client's attention on a solution that absolutely makes sense based on all available data, but it doesn't make sense to *him*, then his preference is to refuse to accept what you're saying. It is important that you see the signs of that and, if possible, look for a different way to communicate your information.

A customer's preference might not even be clear to her. She may hope that you present her with enough options and choices that you will help her discover what she really likes and wants. This is potentially a giant black hole for your selling energy: You work so hard to present multiple choices that the message about your ability to provide something useful gets lost. The dilemma you potentially create is captured in the context of a consumer-goods story from Dr. Art Markman, PhD, a professor of psychology and marketing at the University of Texas at Austin. Markman did what so many of us have done and hit the same confusion: He went to buy a new coffee maker and found a wall of them. Not only did he face more options than he wanted, he also had to fight through a crowd to get to them. He wondered what caused the crowds and concluded his experience captured an interesting tradeoff: "[P]eople want to have lots of options. That gives them the feeling that their choice is not at all constrained...[but] as the number of options goes up, the choice gets more difficult to make, and that can make it hard to know whether you have made a good decision."[6]

In assessing whether you have hit the mark in determining your prospect's preference on price, contract duration, quality, technical support, or any other aspect of your deliverable, look for the following positive responses, as well as the negative ones.

Positive (Your sense of the person's preference is affirmed.)

- A natural smile comes easily on hearing your information.

- You see some nodding.

- The eyes are wide open, not trying to avoid you or the information you are visually presenting.

- You see some excitement in the person's illustrators. Displays of excitement are related to baseline, so keep in mind that someone who has generally conservative moves might show excitement by simply giving a little "thumbs up."

- You get questions that invite you to go deeper into the information provided.

  Negative (The person is sending you a message that you have missed the mark.)

- You see a "Botox smile." It's polite and nothing more.

- You either see no nodding or a lowering of the head to indicate "This is painful."

- The eyes are darting away, glancing at something else in the room, or focused downward so that eye contact is impossible.

- You see barriers. This could mean the person's body is now angled away from you, legs are suddenly crossed, or perhaps the prospect has placed her phone on the conference table in front of her.

- You get questions that challenge what you said in a confrontational way, or statements that contradict you.

Reading the prospect's body language and verbal cues will probably give you the confirmation you needed that you are either on-target or off-target. Use that perception to recast what you're saying. You might just start by making an honest admission: "I can see you are looking for something else. I would appreciate knowing what you're thinking and what you're looking for."

Desire

At the start of the meeting, your prospect walked in desiring something from you. She wanted a product, answers, services, insights, direction—maybe all of those things. You have the opportunity to meet the need(s), disappoint, or ratchet up the desire to work with you and your company.

We all want to make brilliant decisions. We desire to reduce the risk of failure and increase the chance for Moon-landing success. The higher the stakes, the greater our sense of desire. A customer who feels you are able to see outside of market dynamics so that you help her get ahead of them—that's ratcheting up desire.

The route to ratcheting up the desire relates a great deal to you (1) listening during the meeting; (2) responding directly to questions, concerns, and hopes; and (3) observing changes in the prospect's body language as different emotions are aroused by the conversation.

- What did she say that provided an opportunity for you to challenge her assumptions about what she wants? She wants the $a + b$ solution. You affirm that's a great combination, but what if she could have $a + b^2$ at the same terms?

- You tell a story that illustrates how $a + b^2$ has catapulted another client company forward in terms of efficiency. Provide specifics to whatever extent you can. If the company is not a competitor, then referencing their experience (with their permission) would make your point.

- You listen to her concerns about $a + b^2$ being relatively new and untested. Take advantage of the herd mentality to note that other respected companies have chosen $a + b^2$. The alternative to this is arguing that she creates a competitive advantage for her company by being the first in her industry to adopt $a + b^2$.

The mechanics of stimulating desire in sales are curiosity about what you offer, when you can deliver it, what it costs, why it's so great, and why you are the person your prospect feels deserves a "yes."

Summary Points

- Five factors characterize a sales encounter: connection, curiosity, deference, preference, and desire.

- Some people are naturals at connecting with others; some benefit from studying it like they would study calculus. It's critical to learn—or just practice—how to smile genuinely, use touch appropriately, share a little information about yourself, mirror body language, treat the other person with respect, reinforce trust with your behavior, suspend your ego, give compliments, listen well, and get your prospect talking and moving.

- Curiosity results from our natural inclination as people to be stimulus-seeking. You want to ask questions and provide information that light a fire under your prospect's interest in you and what you have to offer.

- Active listening is your essential skill in keeping conversation going. It has three components: intellectual, physical, and emotional.

- The dance associated with deference involves alternating who is leading. The reciprocal nature of the exchange lends a balance and flow to a sales encounter.

- Customer preferences are not necessarily rational, but they are compelling reasons to make a decision. Your conversation with the prospect can get them to surface.

- Not only do you want to understand your customer's desire, you want to escalate it—to take it to new heights!

4

·········

ENGAGE!

When your prospect or client does most of the talking in a meeting, that's usually a good thing. You are likely to hear what she likes, prefers, needs, and dislikes. It makes sense that asking questions is a great motivator to get a person talking, but it certainly isn't the only one. In this chapter, we explore eight conversation motivators, how and when to use them, and how your movements and vocal characteristics support the flow of the conversation.

The eight motivators are:

1. Direct questioning.

2. Offering incentives.

3. Enhancing emotional appeal.

4. Boosting ego.

5. Deflating ego.

6. Easing fears.

7. Creating certainty or uncertainty.

8. Silence.

Direct Questioning

When people feel as though there is some vital or interesting piece of information they don't know about a situation, product, or person, it's like an itch that must be scratched. The more you can stimulate a person's curiosity about you and the product or service you have to offer, the stronger the itch.

Behavioral economist George Loewenstein developed the "gap theory" of curiosity to explain how powerfully human curiosity motivates our decisions and actions. In his paper "The Psychology of Curiosity," he states:

Curiosity has been consistently recognized as a critical motive that influences human behavior in both positive and negative ways at all stages of the life cycle. It has been identified as a driving force in child development and as one of the most important spurs to education attainment.... Curiosity has also been cited as a major impetus behind scientific discovery, possibly eclipsing even the drive for economic gain.[1]

Sometimes the best way to stimulate curiosity is by asking a question or two—a really good question or two.

Your questions should be thought-provoking and focused on a single idea or set of ideas. They should help take the conversation in the direction you have designed for the encounter and stimulate interest in what you have to offer the prospect or customer. A few basics on what constitutes a good question and a bad question will help you shape what you say in your meeting.

Good Questions

From cocktail receptions to formal meetings, bad questions pollute conversations. In general, they prompt incomplete or misleading answers and undermine rapport. On the other hand, good questions contribute to rapport-building and keep your conversation moving in a direction that you have in mind.

According to James O. Pyle, who taught questioning techniques to military interrogators and is the co-author with Maryann of *Find Out Anything From Anyone, Anytime,* the good questions are direct, control, repeat, persistent, summary, and non-pertinent. To describe them briefly:

- **Direct.** You pose a simple question with a basic interrogative. These are the best: one interrogative, one verb, and one noun or pronoun. Examples are: "What do you like about the contract you currently have with your public relations firm?" and "How did vendors who supplied this to you before fall short of your expectations?" Good, direct questions start with who, what, when, why, or how.

- **Control.** You already know the answer to your question when you ask it, but you want to find out whether or not the person is informed, uninformed, trying to deceive you, or perhaps not paying attention. Control questions are about discovery of behavior, patterns of speech, and level of truthfulness or accuracy and they often relate to something you talked about before with the person. For example, you might ask a client, "What can you tell me to help make absolutely sure I understand what your CEO thinks is critical in this accounting program?"

- **Repeat.** You ask two different questions that seek the same information (not the same question; we get to that in the next bullet). You've probably used this technique a hundred times and not even realized how essential it is to your success! Your question is "How many people are on the technical support team?" The person you're speaking with says: "We have 18 in the field." Later on, when you're talking with her about a related subject, you might ask, "How many service regions does the company have nationwide?" She says, "22," which is a way of alerting you to the fact that the tech support team in the field doesn't match the number of regions covered by the company. It's not an absolute test, but it gives you a reason to ask intelligent questions about who is covering what territory for the company. They are two different questions that cross-check the information provided. It's common to uncover discrepancies in using repeat questions, but do not assume the person is trying to deceive you. In many cases, these repeat questions focus on company issues your contact wishes she had thought of! Just go with the flow, show respect for your contact, and display a sense of trust—even when it looks as though the "facts" aren't matching. But keep your notes so that you can revisit the veracity and value of the exchange later.

- **Persistent.** Here is where you ask the same question more than once—that is, you ask for the same information more than once. You will want to change the wording somewhat, and space the queries apart, but you are essentially asking the very same question at different points in the conversation. The objective is to help you explore all facets of the desired information; you are just trying to get a complete answer. Like repeat questions, persistent questions are also useful if you suspect that the person has deliberately not divulged everything you need to know or provided an incomplete answer because another topic overtook the conversation. After a long and animated conversation, you are not clear on why a potential donor to your interactive children's museum will not commit to a large contribution. You have asked the question before about her investment in children's education— "What is your legacy?"—but you ask it now again, in a different way: "How do you want to children to benefit from your gift?" The persistent question, done well, often builds on your active listening and puts the key sales issue front and center.

- **Summary.** You ask a question that is designed to allow the other person to have an opportunity to revisit his answer. To differentiate this from repeat and persistent questions, summary questions do not come out of your concerns about the truth or completeness of what was said previously. This is questioning that feeds back to the person what he has said; you give him a chance to go over the information in his mind so he's confident he said what he wanted to say. You might start off with "Let me see if I got this right." When you do this in a straightforward manner, it is obviously meant to clarify key information. You won't look inattentive or mistrusting. This is no different from someone asking a doctor at the end of a physical, "Please tell me again what the various tests you did mean; I think I get it, but I'm not sure." You want to come across as someone who's interested in what the other person has to say rather than someone who is too dim-witted to understand it.

- **Non-Pertinent.** It's sometimes useful to ask a question that merely shows interest in the person or her situation rather than drives toward a close on the deal. You are giving yourself and the person you're meeting with a bit of pause-time with a non-pertinent question, possibly mitigating some tension that has built up in the course of your conversation. Maybe the question just gives you time to think or refer to your notes. You probably don't want it to be as off-track as "Is it normal to have this much rain in May here?" However, it could be a "soft" question related to the company: "How has everyone adjusted to the new headquarters location?"

Keep in mind that questioning is a two-way street: You are driven to know something, but the person who is your source of that information will probably have questions as well. You may initiate the questions, but don't forget to pause occasionally and let the other person interject some questions of her own.

Be aware of your facial expressions when a question is posed to you. Remember those eight expressions that are recognizable around the world: fear, anger, surprise, disgust, sadness, contempt, happiness, and pride. What if your face inadvertently adopted one of the first six when you're asked a question? There is no doubt that the person you're meeting with would be able to identify the emotion associated with the expression even if you've only held it for a second.

Paul Ekman has a training program to help people to pick up micro expressions, which are facial expressions that occur within 1/25th of a second and expose a person's true emotions. Ekman notes that "micro expressions occur when people are deliberately trying to conceal the emotion they are feeling. They can also occur when someone is totally unaware of how he or she is feeling."[2] Even without a training program like Ekman's, you—or your customer— may sense an emotional response that the other person manifested for just a millisecond. It would be one of those times the highly perceptive individual might say, "I'm not sure why, but I got the feeling that he found my question unsettling."

Flip the circumstance around so you are reading the prospect or customer. If you ask a discovery question like "How serious an issue is cyber security for you?" and you see a look of fear, you don't even need a narrative response to tell you that the client feels threatened by hackers and other threats.

If your brain is registering fear, anger, surprise, disgust, sadness, or contempt, therefore, it's possible that your face is, too. Just be aware that your face may have just interrupted the conversation— and the connection—with the client. Later in the chapter, we look at how to flow into other conversation motivators to move forward and perhaps even get your rapport building back on track after a facial *faux pas.*

Bad Questions

A facial *faux pas* isn't the only thing that can take your interaction off-track, of course. The question itself may cause consternation or evoke an undesired response. In most situations, avoid bad questions such as the following:

- **Leading.** The name suggests precisely what they do: They lead the other person toward an answer. That sounds as though it might be helpful in a sales situation—and it could be if you're nearing the close—however, you need to know when to and how to use it. If you are in the discovery phase of a conversation with a prospect about one of the software solutions you offer, then a leading question will get in the way. You may end up directing the person's attention toward a product that is not the best one for his needs. You've sabotaged your pitch by embedding your own assumptions or preferences into the question. Here is how that might play out: You ask, "How would you integrate Solution A into your current human resources activities?" instead of "How would you integrate one of the solutions we offer into your current human resources activities?" You may have thought it's very clever of you to call out Solution A because it's the most expensive, but if it isn't the most suitable one for the customer, then you may have undermined your credibility and chance to sell anything to him.

- **Negative.** Use of a negative in a question often muddies the meaning. For example, you ask, "Have you never wanted to fix this problem once and for all?" What answer are you looking for? The question could be "Have ever wanted to fix this problem once and for all?" Or better yet, ask a question requiring a narrative response: "What are your thoughts on a permanent solution to this problem?"

- **Vague.** These are questions that are either unclear or not concise enough to make the point quickly. It is very easy to make the mistake of asking a vague question simply by stuffing too much into the question. Let's say you know the prospective donor to your hospital foundation injured himself badly while rowing for Harvard University. You ask, "Given that you know what it's like to need the best medical care, and probably feeling fortunate that you got it through Harvard, how important do you think it is to have great care available to people who can't afford it?" By the time you get to the actual question, you've already buried it in platitudes.

- **Compound.** Listen to any U.S. presidential press conference and you will hear a string of compound questions. In defense of the journalists, the reason they dovetail multiple questions together is because they generally have only one chance to pose a question. Even so, they provide classic examples of awful questions. Here are the strung-together questions of NBC News' Chuck Todd at a 2013 press conference with President Barack Obama: "Given that you just announced a whole bunch of reforms based on essentially the leaks that Edward Snowden made on all of these surveillance programs, does that change—is your mindset changed about him? Is he now more a whistle-blower than he is a hacker, as you called him at one point, or somebody that shouldn't be filed charges...and should he be provided more protection? Is he a patriot?[3]

Even if you are squeezed for time with your customer, don't replicate the mistake of people in the White House press pool: Ask one question at a time.

Offering Incentives

Human beings are more inclined to want immediate gratification rather than wait for an incentive that comes later—even if it's better than the quick choice.

Studies involving brain scans indicate that decisions about the possibility of immediate reward activate parts of their brain associated with emotion. In your sales presentation, if you therefore spark a sense that you have the ability to relieve a persistent "pain" for the client or make a positive impact on relationships with the board of directors, the client is more likely to want your help now. If you say the same thing in the context of spreadsheets or charts aimed at engaging analysis, you may still close the deal, but you've done it by appealing to the cognitive part of the client's brain. For a lot of people, the emotion-related parts of the brain win out over the cognitive parts of the brain.

Remember that we're talking about conversation motivators here. Your ability to stir emotion is therefore within the context of a sales encounter. It's part of your toolkit to keep forward movement going and not meant as a substitute for number-crunching or whatever other analytical exercises are an important part of your sale.

Look for a facial expression of happiness and attentive posture— leaning in, perhaps mirroring you, a genuine smile, eye contact—as signals validating that your incentive has been well received.

Enhancing Emotional Appeal

Use your awareness of your own, and others', positive emotions and negative emotions to keep your contact engaged in the conversation. Also think in terms of a desire for a positive result versus an aversion to a negative outcome or "pain."

This next statement may come as a surprise, or it may not, depending on what your sales efforts are focused on. There's a big reason why it may be easier to get your prospect onboard if he's motivated by anger, disgust, hurt, envy, fear, or anything else in the family of negative emotions: People tend to spend more time and energy thinking about events that evoke strong negative emotions than strong positive ones. It should go without saying—but we'll say it anyway—that the negative emotions should not be directed at you, but rather at the need, situation, or demands that got you a meeting with the prospect in the first place.

This is one reason why it can be so tough for a fundraiser to get major donations from people who have the means and, theoretically, the connection to the cause. Logically, the pitch is often aimed at the higher good, the benevolent action, the grace of the action. When it comes to arts and education funding, those approaches may put you on solid ground. But consider how effective the "Memorial and Honor Giving" program is for the American Cancer Society. You lose someone to cancer. It's painful (negative emotion) and you have a hard time doing anything to relief your grief (negative emotion). Making a donation to ACS has a healing power because the money will help both people experiencing cancer and the families affected by the challenge.

The really compelling factor is the personal connection, however. Personal contact with a prospect has been shown by multiple sources[4] to yield more money that a phone or email contact would.

With a nod to the power of romantic and spiritual love, which are thought by many experts to be the most powerful motivators of all, in most situations that kind of love doesn't come into play.

Maintain an awareness of your own emotional state, as well, and how it affects the flow of the conversation. We have probably all heard pitches from fundraisers, politicians, and people selling everything from cars to cosmetics in which the person comes across like a religious zealot. There is so much emotion present, it's hard to hear the message about the product or service. As a sales professional, you will not motivate conversation with an excess of emotion unless—and this is uncommon for most professionals—you are "preaching to the choir."

Your own deviations from baseline give away your emotional state. If you are amped up, your illustrators will be overly energetic and you are likely pick up the pace of your speech. The opposite will occur, along with use of adaptors and barriering, if a negative emotion—like fear of failure—starts to take over.

Boosting Ego

For just a moment, rein in your cynicism about the value of compliments. Voicing acknowledgment of a person's value, contributions, or presentations is a legitimate tactic that tends to make people more positive about and cooperative with the source of compliments.

Although we acknowledge this is a pop-culture example of how this works, *Scientific American* began an article titled "Flattery Will Get You Far" with the following:

Here at *Scientific American* we understand the wisdom of our readership. Your intellect sets you apart from the rest of the population, and we are gracious to have you as visitors to this website. As someone of exceptional judgment, we know you will be interested in subscribing to our exclusive online material, appropriate for only the most discerning intellectuals, and available to you for only $9.99/month.[5]

Compliments based on valid observations work time after time because the simple fact is this: People enjoy feeling good about themselves. Our brains are fertile ground waiting for the seeds of affirmation, and people who understand how and when to plant valid compliments can gain a psychological advantage over others. When you offer a compliment, watch for the body language of acceptance— openness in illustrators and a facial expression of happiness or pride.

In using your active listening skills, you will undoubtedly pick up something about the expertise, experience, or priorities of the person with whom you're meeting. It will only help you to point out that you place value on it.

Deflating Ego

At the outset, we caution you that undermining your prospect or customer's ego needs to be done with skill and caution. You're in perilous territory if you mishandle this. At the same time, if you do it well, you can forge an even stronger connection with the person because you convey honesty.

In covering "fear selling" in Chapter 9, we look at ways that a deliberate and somewhat aggressive approach to deflating ego moves the selling conversation forward. The essential technique is attacking a person's sense of self-worth, which can enable you to move the person into a vulnerable emotional state and make him more compliant. Deflating ego is useful in more subtle ways in other forms of selling, however.

Done well, it is used in conjunction with efforts to boost ego to make him or her feel better. You bring the person out of a self-esteem slump by following a challenge with a genuine compliment: "I can see how the current program has not yielded your bottom-line goals, but the strategy behind it is spot on."

Observe the body language of someone whose ego has been deflated by something you've said. If you detect defiance, then you risk making the person angry. Your open body language—projecting trust and vulnerability—is important in supporting whatever positive remark you offer next. In contrast, if you see head down and other indications that she is using a barrier to keep you at a distance, you've undermined her sense of self-worth. At that point, you need to give her an immediate path to reconnect; invite her expertise.

These images show the difference between a defiant response, generally requiring open and conciliatory body language and conversation, and one of hurt and the need to reconnect. Notice that one of the big differences is in the way that the person uses barriers. In one case—the defiant client—you are being blocked by physical indi-cations that you are not invited any closer. In the other, you perceive that the person is protecting herself. She is shielding herself from di-rect contact with you.

Not only in the use of deflating egos as a conversation motivator, but also in the use of any of these techniques, the way a person uses barriering will tell you a great deal about what you need to do next to connect.

Easing Fears

When you can mitigate or remove a fear harbored by your pros-pect or customer, you have arrived! Your ability to offer protection—financial, psychological, social—to help boost the person's feel-ing of security and trust in you, gives you impetus to continue the conversation.

In fundraising, for example, a donor's consideration may be how he or she is perceived within the community of donors. What you offer to call that person ("diamond ambassador," "premiere donor," and so on) could make all the difference in the world in terms of mitigating fears of how that individual will be perceived within her social community.

It's more of a bottom-line consideration in commercial environ-ments when the issue is related to fear that the product or service will or will not please the "powers that be." You need numbers, spread-sheets, and other documentation of hard data to ease fears and move the conversation forward.

Creating Certainty or Uncertainty

Let's assume you have 100 percent belief in your product. You go into the meeting projecting that certainty with confident body language. Good start—except that you need one more thing to keep the conversation going: how your product knowledge connects with the person's needs. In short, motivating the conversation with certainty reflects your homework. When the other person's body language mirrors yours in terms of energy and confidence, there is a sense of shared certainty.

You can use uncertainty to your advantage just as much. People feel a little off balance and out of control in the face of uncertainty. If your prospect is in that state of mild confusion—not completely disoriented, but a little off balance—you can move his thinking toward your product or service by suggesting how certain your results will be. When he feels comfortable enough to reduce or eliminate the use of barriers, makes eye contact with you, and shows facial signs of happiness or pride, then you know you have moved him degrees closer to a state of certainty. Again, this technique is part a conversation, so keep moving toward the close.

Silence

Shin.

In Japanese, it's an awkward silence. Your client glances at his laptop, shifts his position in the chair, and looks at the conference room door as though he hopes someone will enter. At some point, he can't tolerate it any longer and says something.

At the same time, you are calm, not using any barriers, and relying on the body language of active listening. Your attentive posture and relaxed demeanor suggest that you are looking forward to hearing whatever the other person has to say—whenever he decides to say it.

Creating intentional silence as a conversation motivator is a technique that we have used doing drive-time radio interviews in which the maximum time to deliver a sound bite is about 10 seconds: You stop after you make your point. Just stop. Wait for the other person to talk because you have said what you need to say. In *Nothing but the Truth*, Maryann drew on neurological research in asserting: "The modern human's aversion to silence can be so strong that it arouses fear. When there is no tapping on a keyboard, no humming of an air conditioner, no traffic noise in the distance, people can feel alienated from their environment."[6]

Your silence is often the only thing that will get other people to talk. And getting the other person talking is a key objective in the meeting.

Using Conversation Motivators

The interplay of conversation motivators in a meeting helps you build momentum and control the flow. Here is a condensed version of how this would work in a sales situation, with the flow of motivators being:

- Creating certainty/uncertainty.

- Easing fears.

- Boosting ego.

- Deflating ego.

- Offering incentives.

- Enhancing emotional appeal.

- Silence.

- Direct questioning.

The scenario is that Roseanne owns a small public relations agency based in Silicon Valley. Her challenge is to get the people in the meeting representing a startup technology company to agree to put her agency on retainer. The two decision-makers are the company founder, a young software engineer, and the company's 50-year-old CEO, whose career had been in household consumer products. Here is a condensed version of how she could use the eight motivators in the order listed previously.

Roseanne sees immediately that the founder exhibits pride and certainty; he looks as though he is already on board. The CEO, however, shows all the signs of skepticism and uncertainty. She focuses on him first.

Creating Certainty/Uncertainty

"You've probably had lots of dealings with PR people in the past and often wondered if they were worth the money," she begins. She sees a nod and the hint of a smile from the CEO. She has nailed the cause of his uncertainty.

Easing Fears

Roseanne follows that by easing his fears over finances and deliverables: He will get weekly reports with the option to cancel with two weeks' notice, versus the 30 days that is standard for most agencies like hers.

Boosting Ego

Boosting ego comes easily because she has a sincere conviction that the business model and product offering are sound and worthy of media attention.

Deflating Ego

She does not shy away from the fact that the CEO would not be an ideal spokesman, however. The company needs a face and voice that projects youth and familiarity with the technology; it is ego deflating, but his body language indicates he is neither offended nor defiant.

Offering Incentives

He acknowledges his shortcomings as she moves on to the founder and puts some immediate media opportunities on the table. She had spoken with two journalists just that morning that she could pitch for interviews with high-profile online news media. Both men now have an incentive to move forward.

Enhancing Emotional Appeal

Then Roseanne evokes a little pain: Their website needs some immediate upgrades to make it media friendly. Can they tackle that right away?

Silence

Roseanne has put the pressure on, and then she stops talking. She waits for them to absorb her enthusiasm, grasp of opportunities, and timetable. The CEO breaks the silence with an invitation: "Besides the website upgrade, what else do you need from us so you can get going right now?"

Direct Questioning

She then turns to direct questioning to take the discussion all the way to the close. She has confidence that, once the two provide all the information she needs to begin the campaign, this is a done deal.

To get different variations on how conversation motivators work, watch a television show or movie in which someone has to sell an idea. It could be a defense attorney trying to sell her client's innocence to a jury or a young man trying to sell himself to his prospective father-in-law. You might also want to watch a few commercials pitching products.

·········

As you observe and listen in both situations, make some mental notes about the conversation motivators being used. Are they being used well? So, for example, you find yourself convinced by the defense attorney or growing to like the goofy guy trying to impress his fiancé's dad.

What kind of body language are you observing in the people giving the pitch and receiving it? Are you falling for the approaches used in the commercials, or are you turned off? If the latter, what was said that alienated you from the pitch?

Summary Points

- Use the eight conversation motivators to help you keep the person engaged and to give you maximum control over the exchange.

- Keep an eye on the other person's body language and listen for changes in voice to make sure you are on target with your approach. Shift to another motivator if you don't see the result you want or expect.

- Remain aware of what emotions your face displays; use your movements to support your mood and message.

5

....

READING AND MANAGING RESPONSES

Each of the Big Four—illustrators, regulators, adaptors, and barriers—can signal the four key responses during a sales encounter: acceptance, rejection, indecision, and deferral. And when you consider the energy and focus behind the actions, you can also get a good reading on the mood and mental state of the individual. You will see signs of emotions that are more subtle that the eight described in conjunction with the discussion of universal facial expressions. On the negative side, these might include disapproval, suspicion, confusion, distraction, embarrassment, and condescension. On the positive side, they might include delight, comfort, hope, safety, certainty, and desire.

Some gestures stand alone as indicators of a person's judgment or mood, but others need to be seen in conjunction with facial expressions in order to be interpreted correctly.

Key Responses

You are always aiming for acceptance, unless you are in an information gathering and sharing stage prior to seeking acceptance. If you have met with rejection and are able to progress toward indecision or deferral, then you still have a path to acceptance, but it may be a long and winding road.

Here are the body language cues to look for with the key responses. They are followed by a look at the emotional drivers that move a prospect or customer in negative or positive directions. We introduce ways to turn the negatives around, or exploit the positives, and keep moving toward acceptance. More detail on this is embedded on the chapters in Part II on specific selling challenges.

Acceptance

Look for a genuine smile—that is, one in which the eyes are engaged rather than the staged smile of a movie star on the red carpet. This is a strong sign that the person accepts you. You should get the distinct sense that the individual is focused on you and is directing his energy toward you.

Open, invitational body language includes illustrators conveying relaxation and connection. Hands, arms, and eyes may have an animation that openly encourages you to keep talking. You might even see some mirroring. For example, you move your hands to make a point, he spontaneously expresses agreement and "I get it" by moving his arms in a similar way.

A person who accepts you has a certain comfort level with you, so you may not see any adaptors, or they will be minimal. If you see adaptors accompanied by a high, positive energy, it could just mean that person is stressed in a good way—excited by your product or service.

People who accept you drop their barriers. They make no attempt to shut you out; they feel no need to shield themselves from you.

As you will see with any good talk-show host, relaxed body language can get people talking, even about difficult subjects. Their nods and engaged eyes invite more conversation and signal agreement. These are regulators of acceptance.

Rejection

These signs and signals are the opposite of those expressing acceptance. This is body language that is closed, possibly jerky because of annoyance or disinterest.

Whipping movements with the arms, finger pointing, and other actions that suggest disagreement, frustration, or rebuke are illustrators of rejection. Another one is any movement that gives you the sense you are being pushed away, such as hands on the conference table that look like they are going to shove it toward you.

The number and severity of adaptors depend on how much self-control and/or confidence the person has. A person who feels uncomfortable when she has to reject someone might have myriad nervous gestures as she avoids giving you the bad news that you have not made the sale. She may even be quite jittery. In contrast, the confident person who feels she has the upper hand might not have any adaptors; you failed to close the deal and that's that.

Barriers will come into play in an overt rejection. You will see the person turn away from you, block you with arms, or hold something in front of her. If you are enduring a slow death with the client, you might see the barriers mounting. They might go from crossed arms, all the way to the person going to the other side of a desk or table before you are dismissed.

Just as regulators of acceptance encouraged you to continue talking, regulators of rejection suggest it's time for you to wrap it up in the hope of not souring your relationship with the prospect. Pursed lips, audible exhaling, head shaking, and rolling eyes are all signs that further words are not welcome from you.

Indecision

The movements and vocal responses suggesting indecision may involve questioning looks—raised brows, a thoughtful stare with brows drawn toward the center—interruptions, pauses that suggest the person is processing information, or facial expressions and movements that seem to challenge you.

Illustrators of indecision could include hands facing upward when asking a question or listening to you speak, as if to suggest "I need more." You might also detect confusion, with hands curling or clenching because something isn't clear, complete, or consistent with what the person presumed.

For a classic representation of adaptors of indecision, start with Auguste Rodin's bronze sculpture *The Thinker*. The work shows a male figure with his chin resting on one hand as though deep in thought. If he were moving, he'd probably be stroking his chin. Remember what we said about the eye movement of calculation and analysis? It's a look down and to the left. That's probably what you would see along with the chin stroking. Some people have go-to adaptors whenever they are deep in thought; they immediately stroke their hair or tap a pen, for example.

Barriers may go away and come back in a state of indecision. When you see movement in the direction of acceptance, try to be cognizant of what you just said and did so you sustain that positive movement.

Similarly, regulators may go from encouraging your speaking to shutting you down if the prospect is in a state of indecision. You may see nods one minute and head shakes the next.

Deferral

Like the other three elements, there is a cognitive process going on, but there potentially a great deal of emotion as well. It all depends on what's causing the person to want to defer a decision.

A prospect who feels a positive connection to you and your expertise, but not to your company or product, may be frustrated. She wants to do business with you, and is agitated that it's not a good fit. She does not want to reject you in a face-to-face meeting and defers so that she can take an indirect approach through an email. It's a passive-aggressive approach to rejection so you may see a fake, sustained smile as the person tries to hide her true feelings and intent. You would probably also get mixed signals from the body language—alternating enthusiasm with dropping energy, moving away from barrier and then using a barrier, and so on.

Another reason for deferral is that there is genuine uncertainty about whether or not make the purchase at this time. It could be a budgetary issue, changes in project requirements, or a host of other things. If you see the down left look of calculation periodically, that's a sign that the person is trying to think through deal. It's not necessarily avoidance of you, but rather that he's giving consideration to facts and figures that you may be unaware of.

Deferral also can come out of distraction. Perhaps your meeting is at the end of the work day and your prospect knows he has to pick up his son after soccer practice. He's professional enough to know that the discussion should be tabled for a time when he can focus on what you have to say. The connection will weaken, with loss of eye contact and you'll see signs of the person preparing to leave the room. When you notice behavior like that, it's always a good thing to ask, "Would you like to continue at another time?" Notice that this is one of those times when a straight yes or no answer is required. This is not the time to ask a narrative question.

Moods and Mental States

There are many variations on basic moods and mental states, of course, but we are focusing here on those most salient to the sales process. When you see the signs of feelings and judgments we associate with these negative concepts, they will impede your success unless you do something to counter them—to move responses back into positive territory. Conversely, you want to make the most of the signs of positive response.

In the rest of this chapter, we are looking solely at the signs of moods and mental states. When we move to Part II, we look at how you proactively handle the negative ones and exploit the positive ones. We give you tips and techniques to turn a sales encounter that has turned sour into one that yields sweet success.

Negative Moods and Mental States

Disapproval

You have concluded a lively discussion with the prospect about your public relations services. She seems truly engaged and even exudes confidence, mirroring your own confidence—these are good signs. Then she asks, "What will this campaign cost?" You tell her what your monthly retainer will be for the six-month program she appeared to buy into just moments ago.

You see a downward pull of the corners of the mouth and eyelids. Her energy level has suddenly plummeted. You see her index finger shoot up. Is she about to point at something or wag her finger at you? You keep watching and see (and hear) her blow air through her lips. Next, the mouth that had the corners drawn down becomes a straight line. She is moving from disapproval to a more resolutely negative response. She breaks eye contact with you, turning away as if to think. She looks down left, a sign that she is calculating.

Seeing signs of disapproval can only help you. You know when they showed up, so you know why they showed up. In this case, the prospect is more price-sensitive than you had suspected. The immediate task is to pull her back into the realm of positive responses; after that, you will address the price issue that provoked her display of disapproval.

Suspicion

Suspicion can reflect your prospect's judgment that you aren't telling the whole truth, that you do not really know what you're talking about, or that you managed to get a meeting on false pretenses. There may be other reasons associated with the individual's experiences and idiosyncrasies, but these three are the major ones.

In displaying suspicion, a person will generally look less energized than before, but the fire is there. He is now focused intently on you.

He may narrow his eyes, even to the point of a squint. The brows would be down in a challenging way, and one eyelid might even be squeezed shut. You would probably see barriers show up, too, such as angling the body away or placing something in front of him, maybe something like clasping hands in front of him or putting his hand over his mouth.

Confusion

A confused person doesn't know where to focus her attention externally. She's pulling into herself with all external signs exhibiting a sense of being scattered and incoherent.

This is a person who probably won't sustain eye contact with you. Instead, you will see the eyes darting from you to others in the room, or perhaps from one object to another in the room.

Vocal expressions might include fillers like "um" and "ah" more frequently than before. You might also find the person repeating herself, which is one way of trying to anchor ideas that she thinks are important. These are ideas that she may be trying to articulate to bring herself, and you, back to a center point that makes sense to her.

You will most certainly see some adaptors, too. Those gestures that reflect some anxiety and are meant to have a soothing effect will show up as she tries to calm down from the stress of confusion. Playing with an earring, rubbing temples, licking her lips—these are all signs that the stress is there.

Her speech might slow down or be halting, too. Her brain is sorting through ideas, trying to create patterns, and that could mean that verbal skills will be impacted.

Distraction

Imagine all that internally focused energy associated with confusion and having it blast out externally. This is distraction: a person frantically looking for answers outside of himself, as opposed to internally. This is the cat following the ant crawling across the floor: She paws, stalks, and swats because the ant is the most interesting thing at the moment.

When you are having a sales encounter with someone who is pawing, stalking, and swatting at an "ant" on the floor, you have completely lost the connection with that person. Distraction can also manifest itself as a freeze response, meaning that they have so much focus on a person, object or idea, that they become extremely low energy and don't respond to you at all. The distraction may be that his eldest son is about to enter college and he's wondering how in the world he can afford it.

Distracted people often mumble. Their deviation from baseline could include a lack of complete sentences, as well as a kind of mumbling body language—that is, they will abort or subdue illustrators. Someone who greeted you enthusiastically and seemed expressive in his movements may shows signs of being less in control and less focused on communicating with you.

Here's another sign of a distracted person: He will pick a stray dog hair off his pants, or she will find a loose thread on her sweater to tuck in. If your prospect is really focused on your conversation, these things will not be noticed and they will not matter.

Embarrassment

A decidedly internal focus to the person's energy occurs with a sense of embarrassment. No one expects to be embarrassed, so when this occurs, the person is caught off-guard. You may see physical signs such as blushing and itchy ears or nose, other results of increased blood flow.

A person who is embarrassed will also probably lower her head a bit and use other barriering postures to protect herself. They might be turning the shoulders away from you, not sustaining eye contact, and just shutting down movements in general to suggest that you need to keep your distance. She also might smile at you, but it isn't the smile of someone who is inviting you to connect; it's the smile of someone who is trying to mask discomfort.

You might also hear nervous laughter, see the person swallow hard, and observe an increase in the use of fillers in speech and adaptors in movement.

Condescension

In the case of condescension, the energy is clearly directed outward at you or whoever is doing the talking at the moment. This person is looking down the bridge of his nose at you, suggesting that you really need to reconsider what you just said or did because it was stupid.

The chin will either be pulled down toward the chest and the eyes will be on you in a judgmental way or the head will be held higher-than-usual. You might also notice the person who shows condescension peering over his glasses or "granting you an audience" by looking away from his phone or computer and suddenly paying more attention to what you're saying.

Positive Moods and Mental States

With all of the positive moods and mental states, you'll want to notice what triggered them, or if they were there throughout the meeting. If your entire sales encounter is a pleasant, reassuring experience in which everyone is smiling, then closing should be a given. You've found sales nirvana; good luck finding it again.

Delight

Look for a genuine smile, eye contact, and lack of signs of tension. There's no need for barriers. Questions and comments will reflect real curiosity. The focus will be on you and the energy will be high.

Unless you've had a previous, positive experience with the prospect, the person isn't likely to show delight until you prove you have the basics: relevant knowledge, sincerity, and professionalism. Note at what point barriers are reduced or removed, and when the exchange becomes a true dialogue. If moving to a particular topic area or making a shift in your presentation style—going to a white board, for example—seemed to trigger the person's delight, that's useful information if things don't quite go your way later.

Comfort

The person is at ease, showing no sense of threat. There is no need to barrier; adaptors are not necessary. Comfort is a relatively low energy mood, but in a good way. If you are on someone else's turf making a presentation, it's possible that she will feel comfortable from the beginning of the meeting.

Signs of comfort include fluid speech, mirroring, and receptivity to haptic communication (that is, touching). The handshake would not be forced, and if you happen to brush against each other while working on a chart on the whiteboard, for example, it would not feel awkward.

Watch out if the comfort level subsides. Remember what triggered it. Was it when you talked about price? Product features? Timetable for delivery? Other people on the team? Whatever disturbed the sense of comfort for the person is a hot button issue.

The Body Language Project offers an exhaustive list of terms and definitions on its website. It's a helpful resource if you want to develop a body-language vocabulary. One of the terms defined there fits into this discussion because the concept of "comfort" does not carry a lot of power for people—yet it should: "Comfort dividend: A term that describes the payback received from building comfortable situations in business and in life in general. It stipulates that when you make your customers, friends, guests, patients and clients comfortable, you derive benefits that go beyond profits."[1]

Hope

We are defining hope as anticipation of a good outcome. Questions are phrased in positive, non-confrontational way. The person seems to be looking at the bright side of whatever you're saying. You say,

"There is no guarantee of success with a public relations campaign." She responds, "Of course not, but you have such a good track record!" Energy is high and focus is on you.

Be careful if you sense hope. This is a mental state that comes naturally to some people; it is their default. It does not mean that when the meeting is over, you have a deal. In addition to hope, you want to see signs of delight—an elevated energy level involving curiosity and buy-in—as added assurance that you are getting through and the message is well-received.

Safety

This is different from comfort because safety means a threat is averted or removed. If your customer seemed agitated or concerned when you arrived and, in the course of your conversation he seemed to relax, then you have eased some fears. At what point did that start to occur?

A person who feels under threat will focus energy internally. There will be a kind of volcanic state in which you perceive that there could be an eruption, but the negative energy is mostly "underground." When you have moved this person toward a sense of safety, then you have established a trust between you that is the basis for a strong professional relationship. What you are offering—and the way you are offering it—give the person a reason to drop barriers, stop using adaptors, and make secure eye contact.

Certainty

The eyes are on you. Confidence comes through in bold illustrators. You sense energy and an external focus.

You will, no doubt, meet with many people who come across this way from the beginning and continue to project certainty through the meeting. That may be genuine or it may be an act.

If your prospect has a rehearsed certainty, it will not change no matter what you do—unless perhaps you do something truly awful and take him off guard. However, what you're more likely to see is a person who shifts in and out of certainty.

When you share the feeling, you'll see mirroring. When it wanes, you will likely see a break in eye contact, with the eyes going downward in an introspective manner.

Desire

The energy is focused on you and what you have to offer. Illustrators are decisive and they punctuate a verbal cue: "Let's get this done!" Stop a moment to evaluate the happy atmosphere. In interpreting desire, you need to know who holds the position of authority at the moment; as we mentioned in the discussion on deference, this tends to shift back and forth in a sales encounter. In short, a customer who wants to close the deal quickly may have a desire to prevent you from recognizing some mistakes you've made, such locking in a price that's lower than she expected.

In general, the desire to move forward in a sales situation involves allowing you, the sales professional, to enter a personal zone—this may be the simple act of handshaking after talking terms—and literally seeing eye to eye with you. Whether you are standing or seated, if your eyes on the same plane, you recognize each other as equals and are in position to forge a deal in which both of you feel good about it.

Going From Stress to Calm

Commonly, people associate fight, flight, or freeze responses with a significant event such as being held up at gunpoint. But different people have different thresholds for feeling fearful, as well as different reference points regarding fear. Basically, from the momentous to the relatively insignificant, anything that puts a person on "red alert" automatically activates the sympathetic nervous system so the body is ready for action. In a sales situation, either party could experience fight, flight, or freeze. The sales professional who realizes he has totally missed the mark in his presentation or the customer who feels psychologically assaulted by a sales pitch could both experience forms of it.

When some level of threat is perceived, changes occur inside and outside your body. If you can identify what you're feeling, then you know if you're going into a fight-flight-or-freeze state. If you know what to look for, then you know if someone else is experiencing that kind of tension.

When people confront a person or situation that makes them feel threatened, physiological changes such as these occur:

- You have little or no control over what happens because after the alarm goes off in your brain, it triggers a chain reaction.

- You start to produce more of the hormones adrenaline and cortisol. They kick-start the nervous system. Your heart beats faster.

- Blood leaves your face and skin, and pours into the muscles. Blood also leaves your digestive and immune systems. When they slow down, it helps you conserve energy; in a real threat situation, your body would be getting ready for the fight or the flight.

- You start breathing faster so you can take in more oxygen. Your metabolism gets a boost. Your body starts to sweat.

- Muscles tighten. You might clench your fists. Pupils dilate to collect information about the perceived threat.

These things can happen—to some degree—if a major client or customer says to you in a stern tone, "We need to talk." They can happen to a direct report of yours who made a horrible mistake with a customer and sees you coming at her down the hall with an angry look on your face.

Let's say your urgent need is to find out the exact nature and genesis of that person's mistake. Your need will probably not be met if she goes into a state of fight, flight, or freeze. The person's cognitive abilities are diminished. Emotions are in play.

A person who has entered a state of fight or flight, even a mild one, will have pounding of chest. His hands may shake. His breathing may become audible. You might see the lips pressed together to suggest he is holding something back.

What you are perceiving—or experiencing if it is happening to you—is a geared up sympathetic nervous system. The cure is to engage the parasympathetic nervous system.

What is the conversation motivator you need to use to trigger a response from the parasympathetic nervous system? It's what we've labeled "easing fears" in Chapter 4. The person needs to feel protected. Unless and until that happens, the person will have a hard time making sense. You may not be hearing lies, but you may be hearing nonsense.

What's the conversation motivator that might be a good follow-up? Boosting ego. After the shaking is gone and the breathing is more normal, you may even see the glimmer of a smile. You've established that being in your company means "safe haven." At this point, you might just want to be quiet. Show you are listening and wait for the person to start talking.

If you see a little nervousness creeping in again, employ the "incentive" conversation motivator by using a little *quid pro quo* to bring the person toward you again.

Are you manipulating the conversation to get the information you want? Yes. But you're doing it in a really nice way.

Now let's say that you're the one who's in a mild state of fight, flight, or freeze. Here's what you should do:

- Deliberately slow your breathing.

- Do something physical. Do not hesitate to say, "Excuse me just a moment. I'm going to go grab some water. Can I get you something?" You need to move around a bit.

- If you're sitting down, order your muscles to relax. Drop your shoulders, sit up straight so your neck is stretched out. Open your hands. Put your feet flat on the floor.

- Put your brain into an analytical mode. Focus on the other person's body language. Is he tense, too? Is he doing anything, deliberately or inadvertently, that is triggering a stress response in you? Are there verbal cues the person is using that are setting you off? Is it the power this person has in your life that's making you stress out?

If you can get out of the room gracefully, then try to find a private spot like the bathroom. Take a deep breath and throw your arms in the air with tremendous power. Straighten up so you feel as strong and in control as possible. Smile. The combination of putting your backbone and arms into an explosive maneuver is called a "power posture." Rest a few seconds and do it again until you feel like your head is clear and your personal power is flowing through your body. Then go back to the room.

You may not need to do this power move because you're already there and supremely confident. But maybe you know someone who could use it. It can trigger a significant state change by replacing the perception of weakness with the feeling of strength. In general, it accelerates a person's ability to alleviate a fight, flight, or freeze response and restore a feeling of being calm and centered.

Summary Points

- Each of the Big Four—illustrators, regulators, barriers, and adaptors—can signal the four key responses during a sales encounter: acceptance, rejection, indecision, and deferral.

- They can also help you get a good reading on the mood and mental state of the individual. Main negative ones to consider are disapproval, suspicion, confusion, distraction, embarrassment, or condescension. Main positive ones to consider are delight, comfort, hope, safety, certainty, and desire.

- You need to pay attention to your moods and mental states as much as your prospect's or customer's. Be aware of what causes a fight-flight-or freeze response for you and how you can counter it.

PART 2

●●●

APPLYING THE FUNDAMENTALS TO TYPES OF SALES

As a sales professional, you keep companies alive. You are the reason they can continue to exist. We don't just mean the company you work for, either. Your customers count on you to solve problems and help them identify opportunities for improvement in their businesses.

How you sell puts the prospect's or customer's focus on the value of your product, service, or idea—and on *your* value as a resource.

All approaches to selling that involve more than one contact with a person have relationship selling as a component if not a primary approach. In addition, the solutions, insights, expertise, profitability, and reliability you can bring to the meeting spark appreciation for your contribution to the improvement of their business.

You are a welcome addition to that person's team.

Each of the different types of selling we explore has some unique challenges. We cover how you deal with these challenges. We emphasize how you can use body language, questioning techniques and conversation motivators, and other interpersonal skills to progress toward a satisfying end with your prospect or customer.

In each of the approaches, the dynamics shift as the conversation moves through questioning, listening, presenting, countering, and so on. The following chart suggests the usual starting points in terms of authority. We also include price-based selling—an area not covered in these chapters—to give a comprehensive look at the strength in position a sales professional holds at the start of a meeting:

Selling Approach	Sales Pro's Authority
Relationship	High
Solution	High
Expertise	High
ROI	High
Fear	High
Price-based	Low

The balance of power—who has the edge in terms of authority—is bound to change in the course of a sales encounter. Before the meeting even begins, the buyer has the upper hand because that person has the ability to grant or refuse an appointment. The buyer also has more authority in the early discovery phase by being the one who describes the need or issue you hope to address. The big shift occurs when you outline and demonstrate your ability to solve a problem and/or create an opportunity for the buyer. That point of highest authority for you might be something you sustain, or it might come in waves, depending on how the conversation flows. Ultimately, though, it's the buyer whose authority level rises at the moment of decision.

Technology can sabotage your ability to assume the authority position you should have during the meeting. Relying too heavily on visuals can make you seem almost inconsequential in the process. You could have emailed the slide deck and stayed at home. Your body language is critical in forging a connection with the prospect and overuse of technology prevents you from using it to your advantage.

In virtual meetings, technology can also sabotage you by distorting your body language and voice. If you use webcams to establish visual contact, invest the money in the highest-quality equipment possible. Remember, too, that body language includes appearance, and that means the appearance of your office as well as your dress and grooming. At a virtual meeting, the visual aspect of communication takes center stage, so be sure to bring the full range of your body language skills into the picture. And just because you are probably sitting at your desk in front of a computer, don't forget that you have arms. Use of illustrators remains important whether your meeting is in person or virtual.

As you now delve into the discussion of different sales approaches, always keep in mind that you have the ability to create value for people, so your authority in a meeting is justified. Your skills and knowledge are needed. Use your body language to reinforce the fact that you are confident, competent, and trustworthy.

6

··········

RELATIONSHIP SELLING

Relationship selling refers to a sales interaction that focuses on the quality of exchange between you and the buyer rather than the price or specifications of the product or service. It can readily be a component of all of the types of selling discussed in this second half of the book.

The beginning of relationship selling is a mindset. It is a shift from focusing on selling something to focusing on helping the customer. As we look at ways to use body language to reinforce your positioning as a "helper" rather than a "seller," we will also explore some common pitfalls.

The positive mindset shows up in myriad ways. A big indication is your use of active listening. When you're the one doing all the talking, the meeting is all about you, not the customer. But when you're in tune with your customer's priorities, your advantage in the meeting is that your ears are open more than your mouth.

You will also find yourself driven by truth and ethics when you focus on the customer. For example, if he raises an issue or describes a problem and you know you are not the best person to address it, you will tell him. "We could do that, but I'll tell you who could handle that better" is a powerful, trust-inspiring statement. It is a moment when a person who does sales can be described as a sales professional. It is a moment that potentially launches a long-term relationship with a customer.

When we label someone a transactional salesperson, it is not a compliment in the context of relationship selling; in fact, it's the antithesis of a professional engaged in it. The term describes an individual with laser-beam focus on exchanging product or service for money. There is a time and place for that, and some people in sales excel at transactional sales, but the occasions to use it are not covered in this book. In contrast, sales professionals who rely on relationship selling—even as part of a spectrum of approaches—want to work with someone over a period of time, or at the very least, have earned the enduring respect of the customer or prospect.

In the fundraising realm, for example, you might establish a rapport with someone who gives an initial donation. But if you do a good job, the rest is stewardship—that is, nurturing the relationship so the donor consistently feels both your appreciation for the gift and a connection to how the gift has made an impact. Your work is to connect that person with something that he values. A common result is additional gifts.

Needs and Desires—Not *Yours*

Whether you are dealing with a product or service or the aim is to secure a donation for a cause, the prospect's motivations that you may not have considered include:

- Practical.

- Moral.

- Social.

- Spiritual.

- Historical.

Practical

A desire to make a practical choice is rooted in the person's need to feel he's operating with common sense, intelligence, and logic. In some situations, the connection is obvious. If the buy is a car, for example, he would care about durability and other life-cycle issues. If it's accounting services, focus would be on the credentials and reputation of the firm relative to the cost.

The need to rehabilitate a company's image could also be considered practical, though. A large donation to a hospital could be motivated by the desire to uplift media and shareholders' perceptions of the company. A company's decision to invest in a corporate jet could also be practical if its facilities requiring executive oversight are not near commercial airline hubs and spread all over the country.

When a literary agent pitches a non-fiction book to a publisher, typically there is an assumption that the agent thinks the property has some kind of educational, ethical, entertainment, or other value. But if the presentation does not make it clear how and why the book will make a profit—the practical need of the publisher—then the pitch falls short. Rejection is an email away.

It can be easy to miss that a prospect sees what you offer as "practical" if you are working the realm of charitable contributions from individual donors. Research from multiple sources affirms the assumption that most reasons that people give money relate more to the heart than to the head. There is one reason, however, that can be very practical: the desire to be held in esteem as a leader or role model. A *Psychology Today* article entitled "The Selfish Act of Kindness" cited research out of the University of California–Berkeley, that indicated the practical, and self-centered, reasons that people give are to retain or gain status, cooperation, and influence: "Those who give more, get more. The most generous among us have greater influence and are, to put it in seventh grade terms, more popular. Whereas, the meanies who are grouchy and unhelpful are more likely to be cast adrift from our clique."[1]

Moral

Instead of buying a car based on price and size, you decide to buy a hybrid because you believe it's better for the environment than an all-gas vehicle; that's a moral decision. It might be accompanied by a practical desire for good mileage, but getting more than 50 miles to the gallon is more like a bonus to you than a motivator. Similarly, you give money to a health-related charity because you want to help save lives.

Morality surfaced as a significant factor in consumer uproar over Amazon's purchase of the Whole Foods grocery chain. In voicing a sentiment Whole Foods suggests was shared by many customers, one commenter on Whole Foods' Facebook page asserted, "This is very upsetting...I want good ethically sourced organic food."[2] The implication was that Amazon would never allow such "moral" practices to remain in place. The backlash over the proposed purchase grabbed the spotlight in the movement for "ethical consumerism," which involves buying and boycotting as compelled by one's conscience and values.

If the consumer impetus to make moral buying choices is clear, do some corporations also make purchasing decisions based on their conscience and values? One of the companies that Jim has worked with is Aflac, the insurance company most associated with the duck who quacks the company name in commercials. On its website, Aflac declares its Fair Purchasing policy, so if you are a vendor trying to sell to Aflac, you would need to be keenly aware that a culture of morality guides buying decisions.

In the course of conversation with your prospect, you may hear moral priorities surface. They may not have a direct link to the company's purchasing policies, but they appear to have importance for the person you're meeting with. It may make a difference if she knows your company has a commitment to ethically sourced materials, supports wage policies exceeding industry norms, maintains scholarship programs for employees' children, and has a corporate foundation that supports educational programs in low-income communities. You wouldn't necessarily want to provide a litany of good deeds and morally-driven programs, but slipping that information into the conversation could only help.

Social

Social needs and desires are powerful drivers because they reflect affiliation with someone or something the person holds as very positive. The perception is that a connection to that person, product, or circumstance is elevating in some way.

A social motivation for buying or donating is strong in many areas such as consumer goods, professional services, charitable giving—most any selling situation you can think of. Whether it's a matter of what you've chosen to wear or who sees you at the museum gala, how you spend your money can give you membership in a tribe.

People making buying decisions for companies may show their social priorities by choosing a firm or expert with star quality. The prestige factor makes them part of an elite club. This could be an advertising agency that had earned awards or an organizational consultant with a bestselling book. For example, the senior executive of a company seeking services in the area of risk consulting and corporate intelligence might want to hire the company founded by Jack Devine (Good Hunting). His competence in the area of security is unquestionable, but so is the social value of having your security needs handled by a 32-year veteran of the Central Intelligence Agency who could easily be described as "America's M"—a reference to the character in James Bond movies coordinates spy activities worldwide for MI-6.

Investing in something like a luxury suite at a professional sports venue also has a social component. In this case, the company is buying the opportunity to create a unique social environment for major customers, partners, shareholders, and other key players.

Spiritual

"Spiritual" is a broad concept that goes well beyond religion. It is about associating with a higher purpose. You can engage the desire of a prospect to make a spiritually motivated purchase by appealing to the person's desire for self-fulfillment. This is a concept discussed by psychologist Abraham Maslow in his 1943 classic paper, "A Theory in Human Motivation." We have a more thorough discussion of this in Chapter 10, but the relevance here is that people reach for the realization of psychological needs after their basic physiological needs are met. And then, if they are successful in meeting those psychological needs, such as a connection to other people and achievement in a career, they can hit the highest high: self-actualization.

Spiritual needs are not necessarily met only by donations to religious organizations, although such gifts have the most obvious connection. Spas and resorts featuring yoga, meditation, and cleansing rituals often appeal to the spiritual aspirations of clients in distinguishing their programs from "ordinary" vacations. In addition, some consumers go beyond the realm of morality in making choices related to the environment, food, arts, and more; the impetus behind their spending choices is somewhat akin to a religious belief. Their buying power is activated by a sense of higher purpose.

YMCA has a unique place in a discussion of spiritual motivations for operations and purchasing. Founded in 1844 as the Young Men's Christian Association (YMCA), organization now operates worldwide and, with $7.3 billion in revenue, ranks fifth on the *Forbes* list of largest U.S. charities.[3] Consumers would book space in their outstanding facilities regardless of their religious beliefs, but many families, individuals, and organizations go to their properties at least in part because of the religious orientation. Vendors need to know that their practices, products, and policies should be in sync with those of the Y. For example, a shared services policy puts some Ys into cooperating purchasing arrangements with like-minded organizations in their area that want to cut costs. At the heart of it all—income or expenditures—is the organization's mission statement: to put Christian principles into practice through programs that help healthy spirit, mind, and body for all.

Historical

The motivation to make a purchase or donate funds is historical in nature if the person wants to establish a significant, lasting presence. "Legacy" is a key concept in this, meaning there is an objective to leave something of value behind for the next generation. Integral to this is the concept of "memorable," meaning that the person (or company) intends to be remembered for making the purchase or donation. This is a potential motivator behind purchases like real estate, charitable donations, or investment in collectibles, to name just a few.

The Citadel (The Military College of South Carolina) provides a solid example of how to engage a prospect in an historical way. The college links legacy giving tightly to the mission of the school—that is, to develop "principled leaders in all walks of life by instilling the core values of The Citadel."4 A legacy gift, therefore, is positioned as a way to leave something behind for the entire nation—for democracy itself—not just your family or the next generation of students at the college.

Although this example is charitable in nature, there are companies that have purchased properties and assets that also have a strong historical motivation. For example, over the years, some major companies have purchased buildings on the National Register of Historic Places with the dual commitment in mind of making a profit from the use of the property and being recognized as having preserved it.

....

This story about ignoring a prospect's priorities came to us from the prospect herself. She was dumbfounded that someone in fundraising could be so blind to the basics of nurturing a potential major donor.

Eileen is a successful attorney who was planning to write a large check to her university as part of special alumni campaign. In the meantime, she found out that the university had taken an official stand on a social issue of great concern to her—a stand that ran counter to her own. She didn't send the check even though she had pledged the money. When someone from the university called her, she told him why she was refusing to send the money. The fundraiser then made three classic mistakes:

1. He minimized the moral weight she gave to the issue. "The university represents so much more," he told her. "You should look at the big picture." The word *should* in that context is a finger-wagging word, intended to make Eileen feel obligated to proceed with her donation.

2. He assumed that her desire to maintain her tribal connections with other alumni would supersede her need to stand her ground on the issue. It didn't seem to occur to him that her connection to other people in her life who shared her view was stronger than her ties to the university.

3. He pressed her on the morality of keeping her word. She ended the call right after that assertion.

Instead of drawing her closer to the university and the positive impact her donation would make, every argument he made pushed her further away. This is the opposite of closing: He opened the door so she could walk away.

The successful approach would have been to:

- Give her a voice for her concern rather than minimize it.

- Revise her sense of tribal connection by focusing on people from the university who share her point of view, not just a connection to fellow alumni.

- Create a reason to reconnect.

The turnaround could have begun like this:

"You make a good point and I'm certain it's shared by a number of alumni. This has become such a hot-button issue in our society that it's important we talk about it." Eileen is now listening and glad at least someone at the university seems to think her point of view has merit. He then adds, "I have an idea." He asks her if she would be willing to post something about the issue on the alumni section of the university website. He notes that university administrators are required to respond to any comments related to policy. She agrees.

His next move is to forge a connection. "Great! When you post it, if you will email me a note, I'll personally bring the post to the attention of the director of alumni relations. Here's my address." Eileen thanks him and assumes the call will end there. "One more thing," he adds. "As soon as I know it's posted, if I'm in conversation with other alumni who share your views, I'll let them know they can comment on your post."

With that, Eileen feels as though speaking up may have been worthwhile. As for the fundraiser, he has now established a reason for email contact with her in the future. She will remain on his prospect list.

This real fundraiser in the scenario, rather than our invented person who knows how to develop a relationship, is an example of person exhibiting a transactional approach. Transactional selling does not put considerations like the five we described front and center in the conversation. The big question for transaction-minded sales people in profit and not-for-profit environments is not, "What's driving him to do business with me?" but rather "How much money can I get out of this guy?" Falling into this mindset is one of the pitfalls we will now explore.

Pitfalls and How to Avoid Them

All of these problems relate to going off the track toward a good relationship with your prospect. You know your objective: focus on the quality of your interchange with the client and that person's purchasing priorities. But sometimes, the lure of easy money, the apparent ease of the challenge, or misconceptions about the nature of the encounter will drive you toward serious pitfalls. In some cases, these problems occur because your expectations for the meeting just miss the mark. It happens.

In this section, we look at the pitfalls and key ways to avoid them. In the next section, we help you pick up the pieces after you've crashed in the pit.

Pitfall: Trying to claim a relationship that does not exist or does not exist yet.

The most blatant example with language is calling someone you have just met "my friend." There is zero authenticity associated with using that phrase, which has the opposite of the intended effect: It puts a person in a defensive posture as he emotionally fends off your false assertion of friendship. Similarly, a blatant example with touch is putting your hand on the other person's while shaking it for the first time or patting him on the back after just meeting. In these cases, it is an invasion of personal space and you will see the person immediately use barriers to block you.

- Avoiding it: Baselining is an intellectual activity that establishes you as an observer. If you go into a meeting committed to learning about the other person's baseline behavior, you will less inclined to move too hastily toward friendly speech and gestures. By focusing on observing and listening, even if your natural tendency is to "friend someone" quickly, these mental exercises may keep that tendency in check.

Pitfall: Trying to claim rapport that doesn't exist.

This is different from trying to claim a relationship when the relationship does exist. In this circumstance, you have a relationship; it just is not a close one yet. A common blunder is to share personal information in a lame attempt to use *quid pro quo* to accelerate your bonding with the client or prospect. As soon as you over-reach, you undermine the rapport you've painstakingly tried to build.

- Avoiding it: Sometimes reinforcing rapport works best without *quid pro quo*—that is, when you say almost nothing about yourself instead of volunteering information. For example, Joan used to fly small airplanes. When she was having her first meeting with a prospective client to do executive coaching, she noticed that he was wearing airplane cufflinks. Rather than say anything about her flying background, she simply asked, "Are you a pilot?" He told her he had just passed his tests and then turned his computer monitor around so she could see an image of the plane he was hoping to buy. He talked about his love of aviation for five minutes; she never once mentioned that she had flown small planes for 20 years. Being a fellow pilot, she got a useful insight into his personality and the way his brain works—without saying anything about herself.

Pitfall: Shifting to transactional behavior during a sales encounter.

You will disrupt the flow of conversation and take your rapport-building off track by suddenly putting your focus on the exchange of goods or services for money. This is a negative result that can occur when you move to the close prematurely.

- Avoiding it: If you have to put this mantra on a sticky note on your wall, then do it: "Relationship selling requires patience and sincerity." Relationship selling can be a real challenge for people who get a rush from closing. If this is you, then perhaps you need to be in a transactional selling role such as a home furnishings store or a car dealership. In relationship selling, you need to use all of your will and common sense to employ active listening so you can hear when the person is inviting you to close.

Pitfall: Countering objections without using questions.

In your mind, you have probably prepared a retort for all the logical objections and concerns that the prospect might pose. You've no doubt been trained to respond quickly because any delay in rebutting an objection could undermine your credibility. Unfortunately, consistently pushing out information without engaging the person's curiosity could make you seem too rehearsed in a relationship selling situation.

- Avoiding it: Prepare your counters with narrative questions in mind. If your prospect challenges you on your timetable for completing a project, for example, ask for her thoughts on modifying it. The ideas might be unmanageable, costly, or just plain ridiculous, but the answer gives you a deeper insight into the person's thinking. That's what you need to keep the relationship moving forward.

Pitfall: Using body language inconsistently in trying to connect.

You've read this book, looked at photos that illustrate good body language, watched some YouTube videos, and you think you know everything you're "supposed to do" to win someone over with your movements and voice. Some of the tips came naturally, like minimizing or hiding your adaptors and removing barriers. Others seemed awkward, but you thought, "This is what the experts say I should do, so I'll do it!" As soon as people appear to lack authenticity, they arouse suspicion in others. In adopting body language that you have learned is open, confident, powerful, and so on, it's easy to come across as disingenuous if you mimic the way someone else is doing the moves. You need to absorb moves into your own movement style rather than impose the moves on your body.

- Avoiding it: In Chapter 2, we gave you the steps to ascertain your own baseline. Ideally, you do that with one or more person's help so you have a clear sense of your energy level, style of movement, and vocal traits in a relaxed state. The baselining exercise should substantially raise your awareness of what's normal for you. You will not only look awkward, but also feel awkward if you stray too far from the normal spectrum. You could look at yourself in the mirror, snap some selfies, or create a little video using your phone to see how you look doing what you're "supposed to do." Pay attention to what is in synch with your personal style and what looks odd.

Getting Out of the Pit

The four negative actions described can happen to anyone, but when they happen to you, that's a pain you need to treat promptly. Here are ways to use your body language and questioning skills to extricate yourself from these potentially disastrous situations.

Trying to Claim a Relationship That Does Not Exist or Does Not Yet Exist

You see signs that your words or actions have provoked defensive movements. These could include crossed arms, throat clearing, moving a little further away from you, crossing legs, or turning an open hand—a hand that has just shaken yours—into a closed hand (that is, a fist).

Give this person some space while you maintain a posture of confidence and openness, and take action to focus the meeting on the topics at hand.

This is a time when you use your demeanor to show some deference. Simply stated: Back off for a bit. He needs to be in charge of the meeting for a while. This does not mean you should try to underplay your projection of confidence, though. You do *not* want to engage in body language that makes you look weak or confused. Even though you realize that you have offended the person with your overly friendly opening, you don't want to look submissive. Avoid the request-for-approval look, adaptors, and hand gestures that suggest you have lost confidence. These include steepling downward and clutching, as indicated by the photos.

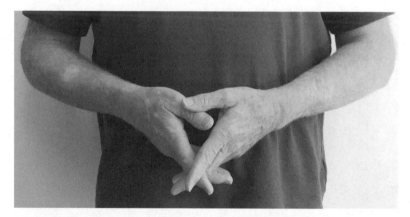

Use one of the eight conversation motivators to turn attention immediately to the purpose of the meeting. But choose wisely! Given that the person has just had an emotional response to something you did, it would be best to avoid an emotional-appeal motivator. Stay away from a question like "How long have you had this Internet security issue?" or anything else that arouses a sense of pain or acute need. You would want to go in a more positive direction, such as "What about the current security software do you think is working well?"

In giving the person more space, you might want to pull your chair back from the table a little. Don't lean back and look too relaxed, though, or you will likely just remind him of your overly friendly opening. You want to use your body to restore a sense that you respect his personal space, do not feel excessively comfortable in his presence, and are a confident and competent person.

Trying to Claim Rapport That Doesn't Exist

Your client seems distracted when you showed up for the meeting. You ask the usual, innocuous question, "How are you?" and she said tells you she's fine, but had a fender bender on the way to work. Instead of responding with a bit of practical information—"If you need a good body shop, I recommend Acme"—you tell her about an accident you had that put you in the hospital for a week. Too much information. A friend would be interested in that; your client is not your friend.

She very pleasantly says, "I'm so sorry to hear that!" but there is no sincerity in the comment. Remember that relationship selling is all about patience and sincerity—and ideally that goes both ways.

With her words, you see signs of disapproval, with a downward pull of the corners of the mouth and eyelids.

You need to move forward, into the point of the meeting, and one way to do that is to say something like "Thank you! Now, more importantly, I hope the campaign I've outlined will make your day better." If you have a report to show or a diagram you could draw on whiteboard, this would be a good time put that visual to work. You need to direct attention toward business and away from you.

As we noted in Chapter 5, one sign of disapproval is a drop in the person's energy level, so a tactic to counter it is to raise her level of engagement. By focusing her attention on a whiteboard, for example, you can stimulate thoughts that have nothing to do with the accident you never should have mentioned. Use regulators to encourage her to talk, to keep her contributions to the meeting flowing.

Shifting to Transactional Behavior During a Sales Encounter

This result is a sign you've lost control. It's as though you were downhill skiing and the slope of the mountain suddenly got steeper. The cause could be misreading cues about the prospect's desire to agree to the deal or your overwhelming satisfaction with the quality of your presentation.

First, let's look at why you might misread cues. In noticing affirming body language such as nodding, illustrators that suggest enthusiasm, and dropping barriers, you might jump to the conclusion that everything you've discussed to that point has been earned approval. Periodic signs of acceptance do not signal 100 percent acceptance, however. Always be sure you ask direct questions such as

"What other questions do you have about our terms?" or "What do you see as the next step?" before you rush to a close.

Also, don't get delusional about how great you were in the meeting. Keep your focus on the other person. If she is leaning in to you and/or mirroring you, you have some signs that you are in sync—that she thinks you're as convincing as you think you are. But if you spot barrier-ing, like crossed arms or legs, or moving a notepad in front of her on the table, then you know that questions or concerns remain that must be addressed before you try to close.

Countering Objections Without Using Questions

Unless you ask questions in the face of challenges to your expertise, product features, timetable, or some other aspect of what you are offering, you are either arguing with the prospect or siding with her. You are arguing if you use statements to counter challenges. By not making statements or asking questions when she says something critical, you are essentially siding with the prospect.

From a movement perspective, be sure you remain composed and remove any barriers. (There is more discussion of how to remain composed in Chapter 8.) From a verbal perspective, you need to introduce questions that invite energetic responses from the customer. Try starting with this: "I apologize. In trying to give you good answers, I forgot to ask some good questions." And then ask good questions.

Here are the categories of good questions that would logically apply in a situation like this, as well as examples of how you might use them:

- **Direct.** "What do you see as a best-case scenario for this project?" You want to put the customer's focus on something positive and to get her to be explicit about what she wants, as opposed to objecting to elements of what you're offering.

- **Control.** You could follow up the direct question with one that goes back to something positive the customer said about your product or service. If she was complimentary about your timetable for completion, for example, then follow up the best-case scenario question with "And how aligned on timetable are we?" or "How confident are you that we can deliver on the timetable you just outlined?"

- **Summary.** Here you are asking your customer to revisit information or an answer she gave previously, so the question could be "I want to be sure I understand all of the key elements. So are you saying that your ideal scenario includes a price of less than $100,000, completion within three months, and inclusion of the next-generation product?"

Using Body Language Inconsistently in Trying to Connect

Something feels wrong to you. You were trying to make an important point and found your arms doing a kind of robotic flailing that was meant to accentuate your message, but instead probably looked like you were fending off mosquitoes. The cure for this body language mess is a smile—a genuine smile that will both help you recover and your audience re-engage with the authentic you. (It doesn't matter if the smile comes out of the fact that you realize how funny it is that you just tried to gesture like Tony Robbins.)

Ron Gutman is a serial entrepreneur and serious student of smiling. His book, *Smile: The Astonishing Power of a Simple Act*, weaves together research and humor to convey how magical and curative a smile is. In his very popular TED Talk, "The Hidden Power of Smiling," Gutman drove home his conclusions with this:

> Smiling can help reduce the level of stress-enhancing hormones like cortisol, adrenaline, and dopamine; increase the level of mood-enhancing hormones like endorphins; and reduce overall blood pressure.
>
> And if that's not enough, smiling can actually make you look good in the eyes of others. A recent study at Penn State University found that when you smile, you don't only appear to be more likable and courteous, but you actually appear to be more competent.[5]

Aside from movement glitches, you can also use other aspects of body language inconsistently. Costuming, props, venue—all of these have to be considered in a discussion of body language because movement and vocalizations occur in a context. If your costuming and props affirm who you are, that's a plus. If they try to modify who you are, that's a problem. As with movements, you have to have a sense of your own style and how to build on it in order to support your message rather than detract from it.

Your body language glitch could therefore be what you're wearing. While working in Washington, DC, Jim met a public relations executive with a high-tech lobbying firm. She wore suits and high heels every day—*de rigueur* for the lobbying arena. After developing a great reputation with the dozens of major companies who knew her through her work with their lobbyists, she decided to form a technology-focused PR firm. She next made appointments with many of the contacts she had made in Washington, most of whom were based in either Silicon Valley, California, or Seattle, Washington. It did not take long for her to realize that those contacts changed how they dressed depending on location. On their own turf, they had the relatively casual attire that characterized technology firms, and when she met with them there, she discerned they were questioning her ability to connect with them. She looked out of place. The costuming issue was so jarring for her that she revisited her business model. She knew she would never be comfortable showing up for meetings in anything but her suits, so she focused on serving companies with offices in the nation's capital.

Summary Points

- In relationship selling, shift from focusing on selling something to focusing on helping the customer. Think of yourself as a "collaborator" rather than a "seller."

- When you're in tune with your customer's priorities, your advantage in the meeting is that your ears are open more than your mouth.

- A transactional sales person is the antithesis of a professional engaged in relationship selling.

- Whether you are dealing with a product or service or the aim is to secure a donation for a cause, you do well to consider that the prospect's needs and desires might include being practical, moral, social, spiritual, or historical.

- There are several pitfalls that can damage your relationship selling. Those to be particularly aware of are:

Trying to claim a relationship that does not exist, or does not exist yet.

▷ Trying to claim rapport that doesn't exist.

▷ Shifting to transactional behavior during a sales encounter.

▷ Countering objections without using questions.

▷ Using body language inconsistently in trying to connect.

- Getting out of the pit means having strategies ready. Some of them include:

▷ Avoiding the request-for-approval look, adaptors, and hand gestures that suggest you have lost confidence.

▷ Refocusing attention toward the business at hand and away from you.

▷ Observing the other person; being analytical. Look for signs like leaning in to you and/or mirroring you that suggest you are in sync; look for signs like barriering that suggest you have alienated the prospect.

▷ Introducing incisive questions that invite energetic responses from the customer. Rely on direct, control, and summary questions especially to re-route attention back to your message.

▷ Relying on a genuine smile to help you recover and get your audience to re-engage with the authentic you.

7

••••••••

SOLUTION SELLING

Solution selling has a traditional definition in which you satisfy customers by providing some combination of products and services that eliminates problems for them. We want to expand that definition, however, and include B2B selling, commonly known as insight selling—that is, you help customers think differently about their situation. In a sense, the "solution" you sell may be recasting what they saw as a problem, or operationally going in a different direction so the problem they had no longer exists.

Despite what some business analysts have asserted, solution selling is not going to disappear tomorrow and be replaced by its anticipatory cousin. Particularly if you're in vertical market sales offering specialized products and services to an industry or profession, you will find yourself doing solution sales. You will also find yourself doing expertise selling (the subject of Chapter 8).

As for insight sales, this is not a new concept. A decades-old example of how a vendor anticipated a new use for its products and services came from conversations between an Apple sales team composed of a sales professional and an engineer and U.S. Army physicians at Walter Reed Army Medical Center in Washington, DC.[1] The physicians were already using Apple technology at the hospital in 1992 when a U.S.–led multinational task force tried to address the humanitarian disaster that had developed in Somalia. The task force's five-month effort attempted to restore order so that relief operations for Somali people could be conducted safely; it was known as Operation Restore Hope.

The traditional approach to battlefield medicine was to deploy medical teams. Technology would have been part of a solution for record-keeping, photo documentation of wounds and conditions, and communications. What the Walter Reed physicians dreamed up in conjunction with the Apple team was taking this one step further. They created a proactive use for Apple's portable computing, imaging, and communications technologies. In the evacuation hospital in Somalia, the technology supported diagnostics and treatment as well as record-keeping. It was a pioneering, portable telemedicine system. If the problem the Army faced at the outset was putting an abundance of medical professionals in harm's way, the solution involved rethinking the problem—to find a way to not send as many. Instead of deploying more people, they deployed gadgets that could record and transmit medical information back to Walter Reed, where specialists would evaluate it and advise the doctors on site. By getting the eyes of specialists 7,900 miles away at Walter Reed on critical cases in Somalia, the system prevented amputations, cured infections, guided life-saving surgery, and saved an immense amount of money on evacuations. A new era in military medicine had dawned.

The Mechanics of Finding the Solution

Regardless of whether you are trying to align a product-service combination with a defined, existing need or to shake up the way your customer perceives what you have to offer, you have to do three things in addition to your research:

1. Identify who the best person is to serve as your advocate in the organization.

2. Ask good questions.

3. Build a great deal of trust.

Identify an Advocate

Your ideal advocate might be very different depending on whether you are trying to match your products and services to a current need or anticipate—and even shape—a change in operational needs.

In one case, your advocate is someone who can navigate budgets and procedures to drive the sale forward. You would probably identify this person through research into the company's organizational structure, his title, and his ability to describe and document the company's need for a product and service like yours. You would also look for expertise: A person in that pivotal role would probably need subject-specific knowledge in order to choose a vendor well.

In the other case, your advocate is a change agent within the company. It could be the same person, depending on the size and organizational structure of the company, but it's more likely they are different people.

Let's look at what to look for in identifying a change agent for a moment, because that person often has unique personal characteristics that outweigh subject-matter expertise. Think of this person as the arrow up-front with all other people around her as arrows that pay attention to the direction she's going. She walks into a room and on many levels you see what the following depicts—that is, an influencer who gets everyone to line up with her:

The body language of the people around her may tell you even more than her body language. Deference comes across in various ways, even among the most confident members of the team. They mirror her. They give her space. They listen attentively to her. If they disagree, they will more likely disagree on a detail than a principle.

Regardless of whether your target advocate is managing a defined project and looking for a solution, or a customer who is a change agent amenable to revising company approaches to challenges, you are better off if you see the arrows line up.

Here's the gigantic challenge for you if you are a research and numbers person who has a hard time focusing on the human arrows lining up: You will make assumptions about who ought to be in charge, who ought to know what's going on in the company now, and who ought to have the inside scoop on company directions. Instead, it will serve you well to pay attention to the people who command response and change.

The "arrow" in front—the one others line up behind—has differentiated herself from others. This is an important distinction that Gregory Hartley made in several of the human behavior books he did with Maryann, most notably *Get People to Do What You Want*.

Some people are differentiated because they are odd in some way. In that circumstance, it's the people around them who set them apart; they don't do it by choice. Other people consciously differentiate themselves from the crowd and thereby command attention. Some people are skilled at using that attention to get their opinions and ideas noticed. They can be change agents.

We did some consulting with one organization in which a relatively low-ranking staff member in a 55-person office was differentiated enough to be a significant influencer. She had been with this group for 10 years and had no ambition to be promoted. Nonetheless, she enjoyed being able to pronounce something "good" or "bad" and have people in the office, right up to the president, take her seriously. When the company's database needs grew exponentially, she was asked to be on the committee to recommend a new system. Donna wasn't the director of communications or technical support manager; she was the administrative assistant to the human resources director. When the committee was completing its review of options, Donna advocated for one vendor over another. Her conclusion: They see where we're going, rather than being focused on where we've been. Her advocacy paid off for the vendor.

Donna was one of those people who could comfortably step in to become the arrow up-front. You might wonder why she never sought a promotion to officially have more power. Her love was music. She spent her personal time singing in choral group and doing regional musical theater productions. In her opinion, she didn't have time to be a boss—but that didn't mean she wanted to be powerless.

Ask Good Questions

We want to venture beyond the basic categories of "good" questions, as defined and discussed in earlier chapters. It's time to explore good questions that relate specifically to discovery. You want to ask questions that help you probe for information that stimulates creative thinking and problem solving.

Jamie McKenzie, EdD, is a consultant on inquiry-based teaching methods and founder of *From Now On: The Educational Technology Journal.*[2] To help teachers in the classroom, he sorted discovery questions into 10 categories. Here we've used those categories as a springboard for boosting the value of the questions you ask a prospect or customer:

1. Understand.

2. Figure out.

3. Decide.

4. Build or invent.

5. Persuade or convince.

6. Challenge or destroy.

7. Acquaint.

8. Dismiss.

9. Wonder.

10. Predict.

Understand

Questions that promote understanding help make the facts relevant and related. Instead of getting bits and pieces of the information you need from a series of direct questions, they invite the person to make sense of those facts.

A standard set of direct questions about your customer's real estate requirements might be:

How long have you been in your current facility?

What do you dislike about it?

How many people do you expect to accommodate in five years?

What are the primary uses for the space?

In contrast, a question aimed at understanding might take this shape:

Let's look at top challenges you have with your current space. What are they and why are they important?

Figure Out

Questioning with the aim of helping customers delve into the guts of a problem means asking questions that require thinking, not simply remembering.

A question only requiring recall would be:

What notable thing has your competition done in this area?

It's not a bad question, but it doesn't stimulate insights about the competitive climate, relevant actions that competing company might have taken to gear up for what it did, and how the notable thing relates to your customer's next steps.

Making the question more of a "why" and not a "what," however, can generate a more useful and provocative answer:

Why did your competitor exceed revenue projections by an estimated 30 percent last year?

Decide

This type of question helps spotlight options that affect the choice of a course of action.

A question that fails to do this just asks for basic facts:

What is your current ROI on this program and how does that compare to last year?

You've already done your homework on the company, so that's probably what we would call a control question anyway: You know the answer; you just want to get it from the source. Instead, use the answer you already know as a starting point:

How would you have done things differently to improve the ROI on that program this year?

Build or Invent

This is a question to engage critical thinking.

The ineffective question about your prospect's public relations program would be:

What's your current situation with media coverage?

Now consider how much you learn about your customer's perspective, priorities, and subject matter knowledge by asking this instead:

Assume you've been asked by Fast Company *to do an article on how startups can get better media coverage. What would you put in it?*

Asking a question like the one in this example clearly requires some level of rapport with the person. Some people who've just met you have a creative nature and would respond extremely well to a question that required so much mental adrenaline. But if you aren't sure this is an approach that would work with the person, just save this kind of question for later in the meeting.

Persuade or Convince

The focus in this category of question is asking your customer to identify prime arguments of a thesis. If the topic, therefore, is sales performance, then the information you seek is what in the mind of the customer constitutes good (or bad) sales performance.

The weak question would be:

Who are the top sales people in your organization?

Questions that get more to the heart of the matter are:

What sets apart your top performers?

How did those traits contribute to your top performers' bottom line?

Challenge or Destroy

The question points to a shortcoming in a plan or an assertion, and the point is for the customer to ponder, "What really happened here? Why is that so?"

The question that doesn't quite take the person into that thoughtful state is:

What led up to the significant drop in sales in the second quarter?

An improvement on that would be:

What issues related to supply chain and manufacturing led up to the significant drop in sales in the second quarter?

Acquaint

We have often stressed the value of all the interrogatives—who, what, when, where, why, and how—in beginning good questions requiring narrative responses. In an acquaint question, however, who, what, when, and where are not particularly useful. How or why questions more easily take you where you want to go. You are trying to draw the person into layers of information.

A flat question that wouldn't necessarily elicit what you need is:

What went wrong with the project?

A different interrogative and a few specifics are all you need to improve on it:

How did the project fall short in terms of time line, budget, and quality?

Dismiss

Just don't ask something that is not worth knowing or that you can—and should—know the answer to if you had done your homework.

For example, do not ask an executive with a web design facility in Bangladesh:

What is your policy on outsourcing?

Instead, try this:

What aspects of your outsourcing policy are working well? Not so well?

Wonder

In a build-or-invent question, you tried to engage your customer's critical thinking, which may or may not involve a great deal of imagination. With wonder questions, you invite the person to indulge in "what if?" thinking. You want to encourage healthy speculation, to have her connect the dots and come up with different pictures. Here, literally, is what we mean by that:

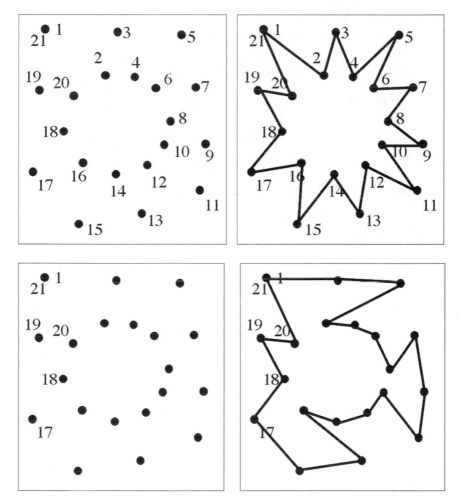

The same configuration of dots delivers two very different images, just as the same data points in a conversation with your customer could yield different conclusions. There will be times when you need to discourage that, but with wonder questions, you want unrestrained imagination.

Keep in mind that it's possible for "image" to make no sense once the dots are connected. That will often happen, but if you are vigorously examining innovative ways to create opportunities or solve a problem, wonder questions can be part of a valuable exercise.

A question that doesn't quite get the juices flowing would be:

How do you see the solution taking shape?

If you want to move away from questions like that to which the customer could give a pat answer, try something like this:

What if you could wave a magic wand and make all those problems you described go away? What would happen first? What next?

Predict

These are decide questions, as described previously, with a twist: They look forward. So you take a question that helps spotlight options that affect the choice of a course of action and give it a futuristic spin.

The decide question we used previously that asked for basic facts is:

What is your current ROI on this program and how does that compare to last year?

The predict question would be:

How do you want to do things differently next year to improve the ROI on that program?

Build Trust

Central to moving forward as you explore your prospect's needs is a shared sense of trust. On your end, you have confidence you are getting the information you require to design a solution for the client. On his end, he trusts that you are as competent and able to come through with the deliverables as you say you are.

Neuro-economist Paul Zak began more than a decade of research when he realized he could not answer this question: Why do two people trust each other in the first place?[3] Previous research by multiple teams documented that people are naturally inclined to trust each other—but they don't always. Zak speculated that there was a signal in the brain that alerted people that it was okay to trust another person.

This sounds like a magic bullet for selling, doesn't it? All you have to do is find out what triggers a sense of trust and your relationship with a customer is solid. Interestingly enough, it really is that simple.

Zak found that activities and feelings that stimulate the release of the hormone oxytocin in the body create a predisposition to trust another person. This goes in reverse, too: If a sense of trust is present, then oxytocin production is stimulated.

Ideally, when you are working with your customer to design and implement a solution to his problem, both of you are doing purpose-driven work. Zak's research documented that this kind of shared sense of purpose triggers the release of oxytocin. The follow-on is that the two of you grow to trust each other more, thus leading to an even better relationship.

Fixing Bad Solution Selling

Solution selling errors fall into two categories, either offering a product-service combination that does not solve the problem, or offering a solution that solves the problem but that they can't afford or use.

A Solution That Isn't

The logical reasons why you would try to match your product and service inappropriately are primarily that:

- You weren't listening to the description of the problem.

- You made an assumption that what you have to offer will fix the problem.

- You don't understand the problem.

- You don't understand the features of your own product or service.

- The prospect doesn't understand his problem.

- The prospect described his problem inaccurately.

- The prospect invited you to describe your product or service because he thought it was something that it isn't.

Let's look at an example of how a mix of these issues might play out.

A company hired Paul to upgrade its project management performance. The problem the hiring executive had identified was a sloppy approach to the "triple constraints" of project management—namely, cost, time, and scope. The product he wanted was proprietary software and the service he wanted was Paul's expertise in helping companies avert issues with the triple constraints.

- Paul listened to a description of the problem, that is, the project management skills and performance of people in the company were substandard.

- No doubts entered Paul's mind; he was fully capable and experienced to deliver a customized software package as well as to teach people how to make the best use of it.

- He understood the problem as it was presented to him. He just didn't know what the real problem was until he had already been hired and came face-to-face with people in the organization.

- Paul understood exactly what he had to offer because they were the products of experience and expertise. He also knew that he was skilled at training people in project management.

- The prospect really didn't understand his problem. He was a numbers guy and so he looked at shortfalls in income and overruns in spending, as well as issues with time management, and all he concluded was that he needed a technical solution to a technical set of problems.

- The prospect accurately described the manifestations of the problem, but not the problem itself.

- The prospect was very clear on what Paul offered; unfortunately, he wasn't clear on what he needed.

When he got into the seminar portion of his deliverables, Paul was finally face-to-face with whole group. His interaction prior to that was limited to one-on-one or one-on-two conversations with a handful of senior people about needs, expectations, upcoming challenges, and so on. When the group came together for their training, their body language gave them away. It was easy to see who was confrontational, who felt threatened, who preferred limited contact with others in the room, who inspired cooperation, and who was obsessively analytical.

The problem was that the people who had to get things done together were not a team, so Paul's solution couldn't be a complete solution.

Part of a sales professional's success in solution selling is the agility of the main point of contact as it relates to addressing the problem. Paul was dealing with someone who seemed to want the entire focus on software and training, whereas Paul could see that the team needed a different kind of help in addition to his technical skills: Solving the company's project management shortfalls had to involve fixing relationship issues. It was not something he knew how to do, but he had seen the problem enough to be able to identify it.

Paul delivered the goods, but he also told his contact what he had observed. Much to his surprise, the executive expressed his appreciation. He said he would do whatever it would take to get his people to stop sabotaging productivity and accountability through their behavior.

In short, Paul hadn't really sold him a complete solution, but he had ultimately thought one through. The customer was satisfied.

A Solution They Can't Use

Consider that your customer has an industrial operation requiring a certain process for manufacturing. You come in with precisely the machine that will handle the job. The customer has made it clear to you in previous discussions that it has minimal open floor space. You have the needed solution, but you know the customer can't utilize it without costly modifications to the manufacturing floor. You are offering a non-solution, even though it's the perfect solution.

You describe it; it's what the customer needs and wants. There is a lot of money at stake. You are not looking at a future with this customer; you are looking at closing a high-dollar sale with a commission that will pay your mortgage for a year.

You already know you are offering a solution the customer cannot use without incurring significant additional costs, so your body language will likely bleed deception. Compounding any suspicions you may have raised about your integrity or competence that relate to the product itself, your body language is now amplifying the doubts the customer has about you. You are telegraphing the truth: You don't mind disregarding the customer's actual needs in the interest of making a sale.

How much are you going to sweat? And if you don't, how will this come back to haunt you?

Solution selling is about actual solutions. If you don't have one, then say so. Or if you have the perfect solution, but it costs too much either directly or indirectly, then say so. Any dishonesty will corrupt your body language to point where an astute person will see you cannot be trusted. Unless you are a sociopath (that's a different book).

Here's how the solution sale could turn into a positive experience with the same customer:

- Acknowledge the drawback with what you have to offer and ask about expansion plans. Be honest: "This is what you need, but I realize you don't have the room for it right now."

- Let him know have considered his situation carefully and still want to help him address it. You might say, "Until you do that expansion, it may be possible to still have the solution. I've recently sold two of these in this area and I know that both companies have additional capacity. Would you like me to talk with those customers and see if they can sell you time on the equipment during their off-hours?"

The customer then thinks, "He's offering a solution he's not going to make any money on." Then you are doing actual solution selling, and setting up a relationship that will yield opportunities for years to come. You are suddenly the go-to sales professional who taps into your customers' needs and comes up with answers to their problems regardless of commission. You have set yourself up to make money down the road, and your reputation with your customers is sterling.

Summary Points

- Solution selling means potentially two things. First, it means satisfying customers by providing some combination of products and services that eliminates problems for them. Secondly, it means helping customers think differently about their situation. Your "solution" is recasting what they saw as a problem, or operationally going in a different direction so the problem they had disappears.

- To be effective at solution selling, you have to do three major things in addition to your research:

  1. **Identify who the best person is to serve as your advocate in the organization.** Identify the influencer(s). Watch the body language of people around the one who seems to be the influencer to get your confirmation of the ID.

  2. **Ask good questions.** Ask at least one of the 10 types of questions that best help you with discovery.

  3. **Build a great deal of trust.** A key advantage in your type of selling is the nature of your work. You are partnering with your customer to design and implement a solution to his problem, so you are in sync on doing purpose-driven work. The mirroring and active listening you do to express collaboration are important.

- There can be relatively easy ways to fix the big problems related to solution selling. Go back to the customer with your honest observations. Go ahead and risk being creative. As long as you are focused on a real solution for your customer, your going out on a limb will likely be appreciated.

8

••••••••••

EXPERTISE SELLING

In expertise selling, you differentiate yourself from other sales professionals by using your special knowledge and skills to meet a customer's needs. The product or service you represent is probably available from many sources, but your expertise is not.

Expertise selling is one component of a larger strategy that would be used to sell a product or service. It is an intellectual selling method that is not meant to be used exclusively. A buyer finds this approach compelling because your expertise comes with something that he wants. In fact, your expertise may be the factor that makes it possible for him to understand the value of what you're offering.

With that thought in mind, we want to offer you some good news the *Harvard Business Review*. An article titled "The New Sales Imperative" opened with a sentiment that should be sweet music to the ears of anyone in expertise or solution selling: The assertion is research from CEB (Gartner) indicates that B2B sellers are wrong if they think customers are in the driver's seat and armed with the information they need to make purchasing decisions. In contrast, the research spotlights why customers feel overwhelmed and even paralyzed when faced with a major purchase.

Buying complex solutions, such as enterprise software or manufacturing equipment, has never been easy. But with a wealth of data on any solution, a raft of stakeholders involved in each purchase, and an ever-expanding array of options, more and more deals bog down or even halt altogether.[1]

Expertise selling is often a good path to get from an influencer to a decision-maker in the company. What you share with the influencer gives her confidence to walk into the decision-maker's office and say, "You probably want to meet with this guy. He has a good grasp of what we're dealing with."

Whether the expertise is something like leadership and organizational skills, or there is a product or process involved, the person needs to hear and see your expertise in action. Case in point: If Maryann is trying to get a company to hire her for body language training, she'd better display her expertise by using effective body language.

Apple led the way in bringing expertise selling to consumers and making it come to life. Their differentiation in stores is making advanced expertise in software, hardware, and services available to customers. They have a solid grasp of the dollars-and-cents value of putting expertise into action by staffing stores with genuinely knowledgeable people. Whether you're at the Genius Bar getting a quick repair or just curious about the latest iPhone release, you are rubbing shoulders with people who not only talk technology, but also show you how satisfying it is to use it. You know you'll never be as good as they are (they're the experts!), but you want to be a high caliber user so you listen, learn, and buy.

All the expertise in the world is useless, of course, unless you have a way to communicate it. In this chapter, we guide you through ways to communicate your unique knowledge effectively to a buyer and to use that knowledge to drive a sale. We also look at ways people involved in expertise selling have failed to close the deal and what they needed to do to fix their shortcomings.

How It Works

An area of expertise for Jim is helping executives determine the ideal organizational risk posture for the components of their organization. An efficient way to begin is to assess their *risk quotient* (RQ), as well as the RQ of their companies and their teams. The concept of RQ is commonly used in investing and portfolio theory as an indicator of an investor's risk tolerance. It also surfaces in assessing environmental issues and in supply chain management. Using it to discuss personal excellence or team leadership is a relatively new application, however, that comes out of Jim's research with executives and teams. When there is a significant variance between the RQ of company leadership and that of others in the organization, invariably there are problems with performance—most notably, sales performance. Think of your RQ as a point on a line between two extremes, with risk averse a "1" on the far left and risk inclined a "10" on the far right—everything to the left of the RQ point is your comfort zone. What exceptional sales people have done through various experiences and decisions is to move that point methodically further and further to the right to expand their comfort zone beyond what had been normal for them. A haphazard approach provokes inconsistent performance; the person has a surge in fear that causes the emotions to rise and cognitive ability to fall.

Entrepreneurs may not start out closer to a 10 than a 1; however, they are forced to have a consistent pattern of risk-taking—regularly pushing the envelope, if you will. Eventually, their number would logically be much closer to 10 than 1.

With that in mind, let's look at how Jim earned a new client by using his RQ expertise in the sale.

A colleague of Jim's was convinced that a company founder and CEO that he knew could use Jim's assistance in upgrading his sales organization. He set up a lunch meeting.

Jim quickly suspected that the CEO did not want to be sold. Conversation suggested he was the kind of person who wanted to be intellectually challenged—to be given constructive ideas that he had not come up with on his own. After an extended discussion about fishing, vacations, and families, the topic finally turned to business. The prospect started talking about his company as CEOs commonly do: high performance, great expectations, strong culture, and so on.

Then Jim asked, "What's the risk quotient of your organization?"

He looked quizzical. "What do you mean?"

"On a scale of one to 10, how risk-inclined is the company you created? And how risk-inclined are the people who work for you?" The CEO gave him a number that was in the middle on both counts. Jim continued, "How does the rating compare to yours?"

His own number was substantially higher than the one he assigned either to the company or to the people who report directly to him.

"What is the impact of that variance in the numbers?"

The CEO said, "Wow, that's really an interesting question."

Jim explained that risking less than your RQ makes you feel like you're not challenging yourself enough; risking beyond your RQ makes you feel uncomfortable. When the people around the company's leader fall far below him in terms of taking on challenges, disappointment will permeate the organization. In this case, the CEO suddenly realized the significance of the mismatch and knew he had to take steps to align the numbers.

That's when the conversation turned and the CEO realized he wanted Jim to come work with him. He wanted help systematically ratcheting up the risk quotient within the organization.

Jim had physically pushed back from the table before asking the question. The push-back was intentional to give a sense of patience and an invitation to contemplate the question. He didn't want it to be an in-your-face question, but rather to be part of a conversation, not a confrontation. The positioning went from sales to advising. By pushing back, the suggestion is that he was giving the person more time as well as more space—more time to give a thoughtful answer and more personal space that he "owned."

He also used a slightly slower than normal pace in his speech. This suggests, "There's no hurry here. Take your time." It's a confident way to pose a question and supports a sense of thoughtful exchange. The natural conversation motivator after posing the question was silence.

In contrast, leaning forward in the chair would have created a sense of urgency and heightened emotion. It would have approached a confrontational movement, so the body language would have countered the intended message. Coupling that with too much energy behind the question would have also been counterproductive, effectively crowding the air space. The expertise would have been the same, but the way it was communicated would have damaged the interaction.

In this situation, the delivery of the expertise, therefore, is worth spotlighting as a critical part of closing the deal.

How It Didn't Work—at First

Eric sold solar panels for residences and commercial buildings. His ideal customer was someone who asked dozens of technical questions. Armed with an engineering background, as well as specifications and spreadsheets illustrating cost-savings, Eric had dozens of answers for them.

His nightmare prospect was the person motivated to consider solar panels for moral or social reasons. He had no idea how to respond to their priorities or counter their objections. Whereas their focus was on environmental consciousness, Eric was concentrating on the engineering and economic arguments for investing in solar energy. The prospects who wanted solar systems for emotional satisfaction thought Eric's presentation of his expertise was excessive.

Eric's failure as a sales professional highlights two traits that people who do expertise selling poorly have in common:

1. They assume other people process information the way they do. It's inconceivable to them that other people are

not persuaded by the same information and methods of presenting information that they are.

2. They have more passion for the product or service they are offering than they do for the priorities of the prospect. The sales rep is therefore transmitting data to the target rather than letting it come to him from the person. The sales encounter is akin to push technology *versus* pull technology: The request for a transaction comes from a source like a central server rather than from the client server.

Eric's sales performance was so disappointing that he dropped his price, preferring a cut in his commission to reporting to the company owner that he was failing. That didn't work well, either, and Eric soon found out why.

The Turnaround Discovery

The company kept Eric, but brought in Joel, whose results quickly exceeded expectations. Like Eric, Joel had plenty of engineering savvy, but he listened to his prospects and responded accordingly.

His listening gave him more than a connection to customers. It gave him an insight on how to make even more profit-per-unit than the company projected. What Joel realized was this: None of these customers had ever purchased a solar electric system before so they didn't know what to expect in most aspects of the deal. They had no preconceived notions about the time or materials involved in installation. Some had a preference on color and wanted blue photovoltaic panels, which lacked the efficiency of their black counterparts; they didn't care because blue held aesthetic advantages for them. Most importantly to Joel's bottom-line calculations, they also had no well-defined sense of what the cost should be.

So, Joel listened in the manner of a true advisor, a sales professional with expertise that was totally foreign to his customers. He responded to their priorities, told them what they wanted to know, and stayed away from specifications they had no interest in—and sold every system for *more* than the company's recommended price.

The Turnaround Technique

As we said earlier, body language isn't just what you do with your body. It is your whole presentation. When Joel was hired, management hadn't made any recommendations about suitable attire for a sales encounter. Sales reps were also engineers who could be involved in installations; they might show up for a call after walking on a roof in the hot sun. Joel had a better idea: If you were going on a sales call, always change into a dress shirt with the company logo. It was a classy look that was comfortable and professional, but not intimidating. The shirt always reminded customers whom the sales rep represented.

Realizing that most people didn't want to know about the guts and wires of a 2,000-watt photovoltaic system, he also did not give a dry explanation of the technical specifications. Unlike Eric's numbers-and-schematics approach, Joel developed an interactive presentation. He would guide customers through it at their own pace and they would ask questions whenever they were curious. When they seemed to skip past something he thought was important, he would use a conversation motivator like certainty/uncertainty to get them to pause: "When I first got into this business, I didn't realize how significantly it impacts the system performance." Joel's technique secured both intellectual and emotional engagement.

By virtue of using the interactive approach, he got haptic communication working for him. Both he and the customer would sometimes be touching the same screen, or at least pointing to the same thing on the screen. Even without actually coming into contact, there was an energetic connection that moved the relationship forward.

Joel also got his customers moving outside whenever possible. In the presence of the sun, he could make his points about solar electric power most effectively—and the warmth of sunshine conveyed a subliminal good feeling. He needed to discuss the slope of the roof and shadow cover from trees, among other things, but the very fact that he got the prospect taking a walk with him helped in moving toward a sale. One of the steps to developing rapport that we discussed earlier was getting your customer talking and moving, so the walk to the outside of the building was part of reinforcing the connection.

Managing Threats to Your Expertise

Among the many events that could bring your expertise into question are these:

- You are now fielding questions that are peripheral to your core area of expertise. You have answers, but they aren't as solid as before.

- Someone new joins the meeting and he's a know-it-all or a contrarian—or maybe a genuine expert with information to match yours. For whatever reason, he starts to challenge you.

- You wade into a technical area of your knowledge and default to jargon and terms of art that the other person doesn't understand. In terms of your developing relationship, this is like a train running straight on a track toward its destination only to be diverted in a different direction. The person has lost touch with your expertise because he lost touch with you.

Your basic strategies for handling these situations are to remain composed and use conversation motivators to get the other person talking and refocused on your core message. These are measures that you have considered in advance of the meeting and are prepared to take whenever they are needed.

Stay Calm

You are the expert, so maintaining a confident demeanor is essential. That's easier said than done, however, if you feel as though you are under attack or have sabotaged yourself.

It's possible that your body may start feeling signs of fight, flight, or freeze. These are automatic, so they are difficult to hide and control. Your blink rate might increase because your eyes are dry and your breathing might increase a bit. Your muscles might tense up. You might even feel as though you're starting to sweat, which results from your metabolism speeding up. Earlier in the book we looked at some of these signs and how to manage them. For starters, in an effort to recapture your expression of confidence and composure, try to do the following:

- **Deliberately slow your breathing.** A great technique that no one in your meeting will probably notice is called pursed-lips breathing. The advantages and steps to doing it come from the COPD Foundation, the organization devoted to helping people coping with chronic obstructive pulmonary disease. They emphasize that this technique not only slows your breathing down, but also improves the exchange of oxygen and carbon dioxide. We're talking about your brain functioning better! They describe the process to do pursed-lips breathing as:

1. Breathe in through your nose (as if you are smelling something) for about 2 seconds.

2. Pucker your lips like you're getting ready to blow out candles on a birthday cake.

3. Breathe out very slowly through pursed-lips, two to three times as long as you breathed in.

4. Repeat.[2]

- **Get up and walk around.** Do not hesitate to say, "Excuse me just a moment. I'm going to go grab some water. Can I get you something?" You will benefit greatly by doing something physical. We have a colleague who saw her boss do this in a sales meeting and thought that what she did was a bit odd—but it worked. The woman stood up and, with apologies, said her back was bothering her. She said, "Please just give me a moment." She was not gone more than a minute, but the time gave her an opportunity to collect her thoughts and re-center herself.

- **If you feel you have to stay in your seat, command your muscles to relax.** Drop your shoulders, and sit up straight so your neck is stretched out. Open your hands. Put your feet flat on the floor. Now here are a few ways to use what we have called adaptors to help you really "adapt."

> ▷ Press your thumb into the palm of the other hand. Move it around.

> ▷ Press your palms together. You don't have to do it for long, but it should give a sense of security and calm.

- **Put your brain into an analytical mode.** What is the other person's body language telling you? Do you detect any signs of tension? Aside from either challenging your expertise or appearing to be uninterested in it, is he doing anything physically, deliberately or inadvertently, that's triggering a stress response in you?

In her book *Lessons From the Edge*, Maryann gave a number of tips from world-class extreme athletes about calming down quickly in order to perform well. One of them works surprisingly well, but the catch is that you can't do it in front of your customers. If you find that you have become so nervous that your muscles are tense—so tense that you are concerned about not projecting a confident appearance—then you could use this tip that, though effective, we admit sounds weird. Go the restroom and make a horse sound with your mouth, or just shake your head until the muscles in your face feel totally loose. We are aware of how this advice sounds unconventional; however, research has shown that facial muscles control the degree of tension in the entire body. If you're struggling with the physical signs of venturing beyond your comfort zone, just give it a try.

Alternatively, here is something more socially acceptable: smile. The easiest way to relax the muscles in your face is to smile.

Use Conversation Motivators

Conversation motivators can rescue you and put you back on track to do a commanding expertise sale. As a refresher, they are: direct questioning, offering incentives, enhancing emotional appeal, boosting ego, deflating ego, easing fears, creating certainty or uncertainty, and silence. Among the things they can help you do are reroute the conversation back to where your presentation is strongest, insert a relevant and engaging story, recap the good parts, introduce something game-changing, and add a brilliant or surprising fact.

Here is a sampling of how the conversation motivators can help you accomplish each objective:

- **Re-route the conversation.** Open with emotional appeal to get the discussion back to where you want it. You could start with "I want to make sure we don't lose sight of your major concerns." Follow with a small ego boost: "You conveyed your primary need very clearly."

- **Insert a story illustrating an important point.** Ease fears that may have arisen about your ability to meet his needs by citing a clear success. "Let's focus on how this worked recently. Last year, Maxwell's financial advisors improved their bottom line by twenty percent after implementing this program." You have succeeded if the short story sparks questions related to the customer's own needs. Paul Smith is a best-selling author and expert trainer on storytelling techniques. In *Sell With a Story*, he gives 10 solid reasons to tell stories in the context of your selling:[3] "Stories help the buyer relax and just listen." This is because storytelling does not sound like a sales pitch, yet it can convey valuable information about your product, service, or idea.

▷ "Stories help build strong relationships." People who know you default to trusting you and they can know you better through stories rather than facts.

▷ "Storytelling speaks to the part of the brain where decisions are actually made." As we noted earlier in the book in covering preferences as a major driver for buying decisions, people often make subconscious, and even irrational, decisions and then try to justify them later with facts. Stories can influence people emotionally to want to say yes to you.

▷ "Stories make it easier for the buyer to remember you, your ideas, and your product." This is a simply a matter of anchoring. It's generally easier to remember facts if they are embedded in a memorable story.

▷ "Storytelling actually increases the value of the product you're selling." Your ability to tell a compelling story about how your product or service affected a company inflates the perception of its value.

▷ "Storytelling highlights your main idea by moving it to another context." This is somewhat analogous to sending your sales team into the woods for two days in an experiential learning program. They understand teamwork in a new way because the context for displaying teamwork was so different from their office in Chicago. In other words, the story you tell positions the message in an unusual way.

▷ "Stories are contagious." People repeat a good story.

▷ "Storytelling gives you an opportunity to be original." If your prospect has been doing her job for more than 10 minutes, she has encountered various pitches, tactics, and obsequious remarks. A story from your own experience, giving genuine insights into your expertise and product offering, will be refreshing and memorable.

▷ "Your buyers want more stories from you." This isn't just about the facts of your business, but also about who you are and what your company priorities are. Just as it's important for you to tune into the motivators we covered in the chapter on relationship selling—practical, moral, social, spiritual, and historical—it's valuable for your prospect to hear stories about how they figure into your business. Not all of them, necessarily, but the ones that you've determined will help you forge a connection with that prospect.

▷ "Storytelling is more fun than delivering a canned sales pitch, for you and the buyer." Storytelling is humanizing. As long as the story fits the prospect and the circumstance, it's a winning way to present your case.

• **Recap the good parts.** Ask a summary question to get started. This is a question designed to allow the other person to have an opportunity to revisit what she has said and clarify key information. For example, if she challenges you on some feature of your computer security program, you could say, "Let me see if I understand how your thoughts on that issue tie in with what you said earlier. When you talked about the security breach...." In this way, you can try to move back to a point in the conversation where your expertise was shining.

- **Introduce something game-changing.** Admitting a gap in your skill set can be an incentive to your customer to trust your expertise even more than before. Always be honest and forthright about what you know and what you do not know. You can take the conversation to a whole new level by saying something like "If I partnered with someone from Maxwell Company on this, you would have the best of both worlds." You are likely to see expressions like surprise and curiosity. The focus can then shift back to precisely what unique expertise you bring to the project.

- **Add a brilliant or surprising fact.** If you are a little out of your element, get back to your core strengths with a fact that can anchor everyone's attention. Make it something that connects directly to the customer's needs. You are using the "certainty" motivator here and you know you've succeeded when the other person's body language mirrors yours in terms of energy and confidence and you have reestablished good eye contact. The body language reflects a sense of shared certainty.

Tips to Buy Time

Your body language can buy you time if you are struggling with an answer, or want to ask a question, but have not thought it through yet. It can also help you keep momentum going while you contemplate which conversation motivator might be useful at the moment.

- Use a gesture to suggest you're thinking.

- Take few sips of water.

- Use a regulator, like a nod, to encourage someone else in the room to talk as you contemplate what you want to say.

- Get up and go to a different part of the room to fill your glass of water.

Summary Points

- Expertise selling is one component of your strategy, and often an effective path to get from an influencer to a decision-maker in the company.

- Expertise selling is an intellectual exercise, so it's important to let the customer feel as though she has the space and time to contemplate what you are asking or asserting. Your body language should reflect that. Don't crowd the person, either with your movements or with an overly energetic tone of voice.

- If your expertise has come under attack, remain composed and use conversation motivators to get the other person talking and refocused on your core message. Prepare yourself to use these measures in advance of the meeting.

- By the time your body has automatically responded to a perceived threat, it has already modified your behavior. It's vital to know how to counter the physiological effect of fight, flight, or freeze.

- Conversation motivators can rescue you from a situation in which your expertise is questioned. Use them to re-route the conversation back to where your presentation is strongest, insert a relevant and engaging story, recap the good parts, introduce something game-changing, and add a brilliant fact.

9

·········

ROI SELLING

Return-on-investment (ROI) selling means convincing your prospects that you can improve their bottom line by increasing their profitability.

Using a strict definition of the term, return on investment (ROI) is calculated using this formula:

$$ROI = \frac{(\text{Gain from Investment} - \text{Cost of Investment})}{\text{Cost of Investment}}$$

Using a broader definition of the term, both the words "return" and "investment" can have non-monetary meanings. Whatever definition you use, ROI selling is never just about money; it's about human interaction.

Here is a classic example of an ROI sale. All over the country sales professionals are convincing municipalities of all sizes to spend as much as *26 times* the amount they had been spending on a particular product. Instead of an item going for about $2.50, these cities, counties, and states have committed to a per-unit cost of $65. Keep in mind that the people trying to make the ROI sale have an uphill battle, because government agencies are renowned for being change-averse. At the same time, using anything other than an ROI approach would be a waste of time. Despite the challenges inherent in the sale, their success rate is high because their case is so financially strong. And then they add a few persuasive non-numbers facts to make their case airtight.

The $2.50 item is an incandescent traffic signal bulb. It has an estimated 8,000 life hours, so based on typical use, it would need to be replaced every two years.

The $65 item is an LED (light emitting diode), which has an estimated 100,000 life hours. Start doing the math: That's 50 times longer than an incandescent bulb.

In making the sale to one of the many municipalities that bought the ROI argument (Boston, Denver, Manhattan, Philadelphia, San Diego, Seattle, and more), the sales professional would have also noted how infrequently expensive crews would have to show up and disrupt traffic while they change bulbs. They would have also noted that LED bulbs are significantly more energy-efficient and provided some numbers on cost savings related to electricity. Then there are other "soft" ROI factors such as the reliability and predictability, both of which are important for public safety. This is where human interaction would come into play as the vendor would cite instances in which cars collided or ambulances were blocked due to a failed signal.

No matter how many factors you throw in to the ROI sell, the compelling argument is that the municipality will definitely save money in the long run by converting to LED. The other factors fuel the conversation and engage the emotion of the buyer, but the winning argument is about money.

In contrast to this scenario, ROI selling is not always able to throw a bucket of cold water on the old way of doing things. And it isn't always able to offer a hot spring of cost-savings and/or profitability with the new way of doing things. It's usually more complicated than that. For one thing, your projections on savings or profitability will not be precisely accurate unless you are in the uncommon situation of having abundant, detailed information from the prospect. As a corollary, your best numbers will probably be a range rather than specific numbers. In ROI selling, too much specificity can undermine your assertions about the value of your product or service.

Ironically, ROI selling is a subjective process even though ROI itself is a numbers-based concept. People often feel driven to buy for reasons that have little to do with facts—intuition, personal preference, and so on—and then attempt to justify the choice with facts later. In a meeting with you, therefore, they might not be totally honest about their criteria for a decision, because they haven't sorted them out in their own mind. And when you're trying to convert a prospect to a customer, you may try to beef up your facts so they have emotional appeal. You rationalize that estimating returns on the high side of what's possible is more enticing than giving a conservative set of results. This is not an evil plot to deceive the prospect; a surge of optimism has colored your presentation. In short, both parties can have motives and opportunity to manipulate the truth with the endgame in mind.

Something as simple, and relatively innocent, as giving an off-handed response to a question can trigger the body language of deception. For example, you ask your prospect about the maintenance costs of the system he has now and is looking to replace. He is not quite sure, but wants to keep the conversation moving ahead so he throws out a number. You look at him quizzically; this is an area you know well and the number seems low. He realizes he must have given you bad information; technically speaking, that's a lie. He suddenly feels bad about what he did and starts brushing non-existent lint off the cuff of his jacket. That's an adaptor caused by stress—and the stress was induced by the embarrassment of not being fully truthful.

For reasons like these, the chapter features insights on the body language of deception. As part of that discussion, you will see how body language can tie in with verbal signals that tell you information is missing, exaggerated, or misrepresented. You will also find insights as to how the body language of deception—yours and the client's—might show up in the context of ROI selling.

If you can spot glitchy behavior, you can do something to bring the discussion back to the cold, hard facts—that is, the money your customer will save or make as a result of doing business with you. The process starts with accurate information. Without it, any ROI you calculate will be wrong.

We also take a look at ways of envisioning "return" that can get your prospect emotionally charged up. For example, in the realm of return on marketing investment (ROMI), the promise of a return like "increased customer loyalty" could be the most important thing on her mind. When you make your case for being able to deliver that, and she responds with the body language of acceptance, it's time to close.

Looking for a (White) Lie

We don't want to be harsh in using the term *lie,* because the chances are much greater that a variation on the truth that comes out in a meeting is inadvertent. Neither you nor your prospect walked into the room with a scheme to engage in blatant deception. That's the stuff of con artists, not sales professionals. (This is not a book for con artists.)

What we call a lie is something that is said, or not said, that alters a fact. Intentionally rounding your estimate on the cost-savings related to a product from 40–45 percent to 45–50 percent is an exaggeration; therefore, it is technically a lie. Regardless of how reasonable it is, or whatever justification you have for providing that number, your body knows that what just came out of your mouth isn't consistent with what you calculated—and your body is likely to produce a stress response. When you both spot these stress responses and feel that you yourself are experiencing them, you have a vastly improved ability to have a constructive conversation that builds trust.

The Whole Picture

In any conversation about body language, it's easy to focus on the puzzle pieces and never see the completed puzzle.

Earlier in the book, we described a number of pieces: facial expressions, eye movement, nervous ticks, shift in energy, and more. Awareness of them is essential for determining a person's baseline. Keeping your eyes on them can clue you in to a deviation from baseline. In other words, when you see variances in energy, gestures that are unusual for the person, or a number of specific facial expressions and eye movements, you are detecting some level of stress. You don't know if the stimulus is good or bad; sensing that you are about to make a huge commission on a deal will cause a "good stress" response.

When you spot stress, you can potentially spot deception, as lying to any degree tends to arouse a stress response from normal people. But the individual deviations from what you perceived as baseline behavior may not indicate deception; you need to put the puzzle pieces together to figure that out. When you're in a meeting with a prospect, make sure you do two things when you notice a stress response:

1. Step back (figuratively or literally) and look at the whole person. Keep in mind culture, as well as the habits and quirks you picked up during baselining.

2. Ask yourself, "Why? Why is this person manifesting stress *now?*"

The Pieces and Parts

With these thoughts in mind, here are some specific indicators of discomfort that should make you look for more evidence that they suggest there is something wrong with what you've just been told, or are about to be told.

Forehead

The forehead has a surprisingly broad range of abilities. By lowering the head you can gaze up at someone and look skeptical—or seductive, depending on what your eyebrows are doing. By wrinkling it, you can look quizzical, confused, or deranged. In the context of our look at deception, let's focus on the action of the eyebrows and the grief muscles, which are between your eyebrows.

Do you see eyebrows shoot up? If you don't detect surprise, which is one of the eight universal expressions easily identified by people around the world, then you may see a look of uncertainty. The person's speech and face are implying question marks, regardless of whether or not he's asking a question. If you had to write a caption for the photo of this face, it would be "You believe me, don't you?"

This request-for-approval expression could occur after you ask a direct question, such as "How satisfied were you with your brand-building program last year?" What he says may be subjective: "We thought the program was powerful." Inside, he's thinking about how the numbers didn't add up based on what it cost the company, so the statement is delivered with a question mark on his face. He wants you to believe him, even though he doesn't believe himself.

Another clear signal that something is wrong is use of the grief muscles. These are two muscles in the center of the forehead that you rub when you're stressed out. They will contract on a person who has genuine concern about a person, an event, or something she said. A person who told you something in an effort to deceive you—even just a little bit—might contract the grief muscles. For example, a prospect who respects what you have to offer and wants to work with you might "fudge" the company's willingness and ability to pay your standard fee. The prospect is a person of integrity and her distortion of the truth is painful to her. It shows up in her forehead. If you see her rub that area, you have even stronger confirmation that she's in pain over what she said to you.

In these cases, the brow is an illustrator—one of the Big Four. Again, we are talking about a movement that accentuates the message a person is conveying. In these instances, the message is not articulating it in words, although the person is still conveying it. Your prospect is not telling you the whole truth, not answering the question you asked—but the truth is circulating around in her head and that causes the stress responses in the forehead.

Eyes

Eye movement gives us rich insights into a person's thoughts and emotions. Imagine the inside of your brain, with a portion devoted to seeing, another portion devoted to hearing, and so on. When you're trying to remember a fact or imagine a solution to a problem, your eyes move as though they are exploring the interior of your mind. And if your eyes are really directed toward another person, that eye contact suggests your mental focus is on that individual.

A signal that your connection with someone has experienced an interruption is when the person breaks eye contact with you after you ask a question. (This can work in reverse, so check yourself out, too!) Which way are the eyes moving?

- If the eyes go up to the left or up to the right, remember what you learned from baselining him. One direction is his recall side, and the other, imagination.

- If the eyes go down left, it's a sign there is calculation going on. In a meeting on ROI, this is something you're very likely to see when you're talking numbers.

- If the eyes go down right, however, that suggests an emotional response. Why would someone have an emotional reaction to a question about numbers? Why would a question about numbers cause pain?

Another possible sign of deception involves touching a closed eye or just closing the eyes. Remember how you thought you could make people go away when you were a kid just by putting your hands over your eyes? Maybe you don't because this is something very small children do. Adults sometimes carry over that behavior and will cover an eye or shut one or both eyes because they told you something that wasn't quite true and are embarrassed about it. They want to make you "go away." Averting the eyes with a downward or sideward glance will do the same thing.

Here is a tip about whether or not the person you are meeting with has doubts about what you have said: A clue as to how your client is responding to you, your information, or the situation is the whites of her eyes. Wide-open eyes, with lots of white (sclera) visible, signals a need to take in more information. The driving emotion could be curiosity, surprise, or fear. In all of those states, the overriding impulse is to learn more. In contrast, if the eyes narrow, thereby reducing the white, she could be angry or highly skeptical that what you just said is true.

Temples

The temple is the side of the head, just past the eyes. Tension headaches often settle there, which is why you may see people under stress rub their temples.

Temples also play a role in expression joy and pleasure. The wrinkles of a genuine smile are what we know as crow's feet—a sure sign that you have engaged the orbicularis oculi muscles.

In contrast, a fake smile is a cover-up unless Botox is involved. (Botox is an injected drug that temporarily paralyzes muscles and is used on various parts of the face to counter wrinkles.) The person offering you a fake smile is relying solely on a different set of muscles, the zygomatic muscles, which are easily controllable muscles near the mouth. If you see the mouth smiling, but not the eyes, the person is not being honest with you. Look for brow movement that reinforces your assessment that the smile is a disguise for concern, disbelief, anger, or another emotion.

Face

Changes in skin color on the face offer excellent insights into a person's mental state. If a person is in a state of fight or flight, for example, blood moves the muscles that need to run or do battle, so the complexion becomes pallid.

Blushing is another involuntary stress response, unless it's suddenly gotten very warm in the room where you're meeting. Many people blush when they are embarrassed. Awareness that they've lied—and, yes, exaggeration and omission of facts are types of lies—is a source of embarrassment for generally honest people.

Nose and Ears

There is a lot of blood flow to the nose and ears, and emotions, exercise, and temperature are just a few of the factors that can increase that flow.

Sometimes a person touches her nose or ears for the same reason a cat scratches its ear: it itches. Other times, it indicates sudden blood flow to the area—an involuntary stress response. In that case, there is a stress-related reason why the nose itches at that moment.

Ears are associated with a great many adaptors—those gestures that you do when you feel anxious. They are a sensitive part of the body, so it's natural to stroke or tug them when you feel the slightest bit nervous. Often you will find women with pierced ears fiddling with an earring when they feel some stress. Knowing this, if you see some ear-focused behavior during your meeting, you should wonder what caused it. Either something about the conversation is causing tension or your client habitually plays with her earring. If you base-lined well, you will be able to spot the behavioral change.

Here is something that you should keep in mind as a professional in sales: Touching your face is generally construed as a nervous gesture. It doesn't matter if the people you're meeting with have studied body language or not. When you touch your face, subliminally others in the meeting have a negative response. This will work against you particularly when you are trying to get buy-in. You will convey a more honest and open impression if you just keep your hands off your face.

Mouth

Many people have been credited with the thought that "The eyes are the windows to the soul." Although that may be true, the mouth is the window to the internal dialogue.

Pursed lips, or lips drawn into the mouth as in the photo, suggest the person is holding words—and possibly emotions—back. After you see this, listen for the pace and pitch of what is said next. Is the speech halting or slower? Do you hear a change in pitch, whether higher or lower? And if you see it after the person has just responded to your question, you might wonder whether or not you received a complete answer to it. Note well: As someone in sales, how often have you given a partial answer to a question—maybe just delivering the positive vision instead of the complete picture? The next time you are about to do that, or have just done it, pay attention to what your mouth is doing.

Another action to watch for is covering the mouth, a sign of the need for protection or secrecy.

Neck and Shoulders

The neck is an especially vulnerable area of the body containing major vessels like the jugular vein and carotid artery. There is a natural instinct to protect it and when people are nervous you will see the hand go toward the notch in the neck. Women will commonly put a hand toward the neck in a protective gesture, and men who are wearing a tie will adjust the tie. Consider the opposite gesture for a moment: If a person exposes his or her neck, that's a sign of trust or even submission.

Some people automatically put tension into the neck and shoulders. Their jaw clenches slightly. The neck muscles become taut. The shoulders rise a bit. When Maryann was in college, her friends used to tease her about this: "Whenever it's your turn to make dinner, your shoulders are in your jawbones when you're at the stove!" This is the kind of automatic response to tension that stays with us for life. We can raise our awareness of it and practice relaxation techniques, but when it comes to the moment when stress sets in, we tend to default.

Watch for these neck and shoulder responses after a question. If you see them, then conclude that the answer has emotion behind it. Ask yourself why. One answer could be that your prospect had never thought of that question before. Another is that she didn't want to answer that question. Yet another is that she expected the question and has prepared an answer that is not completely truthful. Three very different scenarios.

Squared shoulders generally project authority, confidence, and precision. This is why military organizations require this posture. It can also mean the person is feeling insecure, however. Go back to the individual's baseline. A person's whose normal bearing does not include squared shoulders could be adopting that posture because he's feeling uncertain about what he said or did and is overcompensating.

Take it a degree or two further. Squared shoulders present the image of being battle-ready, so a person who is so insecure that he feels threatened may square off as part of a fight-or-flight response. If you challenged the person's facts or logic, even though you meant it as part of a productive conversation, you may have put the person into a defensive mode.

Arms and Hands

Arms and hands do a number of fascinating things together. They can serve as weapons, conveyors of affection, invitations into personal space, descriptors of objects and events, and defenders of personal safety.

Watch for hands to go from open to closed, for fidgeting fingers, or for a prop to be suddenly necessary (a pen, a phone, a paper clip). What provoked the response: a question or a statement? The abrupt change isn't necessarily negative. It could just mean that you incited some thinking and your client has a lot of internal mental energy around what you just said.

But look closely: An abrupt change in arm position such as an open arm position to movement close to the torso, and perhaps crossed arms over the torso, can suggest discomfort. Depending on what the face and eyes are doing, of course, these movements could also suggest boredom. This is one of those many times when your preliminary conclusions cannot be based on a single gesture.

A more extreme version of the arm cross that does send a distinct signal is gripping the arms or tucking them in tightly after crossing them. The barrier is in place; at the moment, you and you ideas are not coming any closer to that client.

The discussion of arms and hands as co-conspirators in deception would not be complete with a note about batoning. *Batoning* is a movement in which the arm and hand are used like a conductor's baton. The classic example is former President Bill Clinton's use of it in his denial of having a sexual relationship with Monica Lewinsky. His hand and arm went up and down in an effort to accentuate his message—which, of course, was false.

Batoning is not always associated with deception, but if you see it used to emphasize a statement that you already suspect has holes in it, then it's a red flag.

Legs and Feet

Our awareness of what our legs and feet are doing is often quite limited. We might feel in control of the body parts closer to the brain, like the hands and arms, but those parts below the waist sometimes seem to belong to a different person. We had personal experience with the CEO of a major multi-national company whose legs often shook uncontrollably when he was emotionally charged. Even after being reminded of this, he could not change his behavior. His strategy was to sit behind a desk or with his legs under a table to hide the problem, but he could not seem to make the problem itself go away. Let this be a reminder that legs and feet sometimes signal feelings and mental states more candidly than other body parts.

If the person is seated, crossing legs can be a subconscious way of throwing up a barrier. Look for other signs that he might feel a need for a barrier. Crossed legs sometimes mean nothing more than "this is how I make myself comfortable." When you baselined the person, this is a distinction that may have become apparent.

Crossing ankles is generally a different message, by the way. It's more a signal of feeling parked in a particular spot, with one possible meaning being "The meeting isn't over yet."

Be careful about making assumptions when you see a jiggling foot. For some people it is an adaptor, therefore a sign of stress. For many others, however, it's just a sign of excess energy. This can be part of someone's baseline; she's revved up much of the time.

What if you notice that your prospect has his feet pointed toward the door? It could be that his subconscious is trying to lead his entire body toward the door. Ask yourself what happened that would cause him to want to leave the room.

Vocalics

To recap what we introduced in Chapter 2, vocalics is an area of non-verbal communication studies because it's about how something is said rather than what is being said. The changes you hear in the characteristics of a person's voice as well as the use of fillers like "um" and "ah" are part of the whole picture. If those vocal patterns or traits deviate sharply from what is normal for the person, then make a mental note. What was the question or comment that seemed to provoke that change?

Go a little deeper in your analysis now—a little deeper into your gut feeling, that is. Would you describe the vocal change as thoughtful, confused, antagonistic, angry, delighted? You name the response that you think pegs the mental state. Combine that judgment with what you have observed about the body language to ascertain what that person is likely thinking and feeling.

Looking for Trust

When someone believes you have the product, service, process, or model that delivers an impressive return on investment, you have inspired trust. Now you need to make sure you can spot it because, when you do, it's time to close the deal.

Return and Investment

Although we began the chapter with the classic ROI formula, the meaning of the terms *return* and *investment* have taken on new dimensions for many people in business. With that in mind, consider how the determination of a good return could mean that the client is interested in far more than a healthy profitability. Similarly, the concept of investment can have different meanings depending on context. In a return-on-marketing-investment model, for example, the investment is logged as marketing spending that has been risked as opposed to money that is tied up in tangibles.

As a precursor to looking at management and mismanagement of the critical factors in ROI selling, consider the variations possible on the meanings of "return" and "investment."

We all know the definition of "return" that relates to profit: numbers you can log on a spreadsheet. But the return that a major corporate donor gets for an investment in an art museum is concurrently difficult to measure and necessary to measure. If your ROI selling involves a fluid or subjective definition of return, then you have more emotions coming to the meeting that you would in conventional ROI selling.

And when emotions come into the room with your prospect, then your skill in observing body language is essential. You can try to "win" on the numbers, but strength of your position is just as we described in relationship selling: It's a matter of how much trust you can build.

ROI is used in many ways and contexts. To some extent, it has become a catch-all for any positive outcome. Though we started this chapter with both a strict and a broad definition, there are many more uses. Here are some ways that the concept of ROI enters into the discussion in a social media context.

Peter Friedman has overseen hundreds of successful social media programs including Apple's industry wide social network. His categorization of types, and relative merits, of return in a social media context show the scope and meaning of "return" to marketing professionals. Friedman suggests five classes of ROI:[1]

1. **Social media statistics ROI.** This is a tough one because the statistics alone do not give a true picture of the return. If you have 1,000 people commenting on a blog post about your new product and 800 of them are about the political orientation of the company CEO, you have great statistics with negligible return.

2. **Marketing statistics ROI.** The company is trying to drive awareness, using social media to get you to pay attention to the brand. If you're selling this concept to a company, you need buy-in on the assertion that this is a cost-effective means of outreach.

3. **Learning ROI.** The big return can be getting a giant, global, virtual focus group to exchange thoughts on a product or service. Just as with the others, part of the data involves numbers of people or posts, but the return is so much more than the numbers.

4. **Relationship-building ROI.** In this category, social media supports a company's desire to connect meaningfully with customers and measure their intent to buy. Friedman notes that the big return is sweet: "Here you're getting into the deepest potential ROI: enhanced customer relationships which ultimately become sustainable sales ROI. Relationship-building stats include increased customer loyalty, brand advocacy, and intent to buy."[2]

5. **Sales ROI.** This category is the big winner in terms of measureable return. According to Friedman:

> There are two kinds of sales ROI from social media. There's the direct revenue lift brands see when they push promotions through social. This is a hard ROI—but it's limited compared to long-term sales ROI generated from relationship-building ROI when customers become active with the brand community, form a deeper relationship, and build a space for the brand and its products in their and their friends' everyday lives. Here is where we see increased loyalty, increased lifetime customer value, and enhanced revenue growth that's sustained over time.[3]

In defining "investment," we are talking primarily about money. However, money is rarely isolated from other considerations such as time line, the degree to which tying up the money affects other needs, and the size of the investment in relation to available working capital. There is also an emotional component in some cases. For example, if the company your prospect founded just last year is considering a major capital investment, then it's possible he is infused with optimism, fear, confusion, curiosity, and a host of other emotions. The investment will never be "just" about the money.

Success With Critical Factors

If you are at the point with your prospect that you are looking for signs of acceptance, you have succeeded in managing two critical factors in any ROI selling: clarifications on "return" and on "investment." You accomplished:

- Getting the answer to the question "This is a good return relative to *what?*"

- Gaining a firm understanding of your prospect's relationship to his investment.

Relative to What?

In getting the answer to the question "This is a good return relative to *what?*" you had to combine homework done prior to the meeting with strong rapport. Among other things, the rapport should give you the hurdle rate—that is, the minimum rate the company expects to earn as a result of investing in a product or project. Rapport should also yield insights about business dealings that have made your prospect delighted in the past, as well as those that have disappointed him. As a corollary, you know the scope of his definition of the word *return*—whether it's "just" money, money that brings with it other non-monetary rewards, or both.

A few years ago, the development officer for a new children's museum approached the chair of the city council and asked her to introduce a proposal for annual city funding for the museum. On the surface, the return would be a boost to the chair's political capital—the goodwill that would get her re-elected. But there were lots of things the chair could do to generate goodwill. Why was this action any better? The return the development officer described took her breath away: The museum was located in the poorest city neighborhood, which was where she grew up. The funding would provide daily, after-school learning programs for every child in that neighborhood who wanted to participate. The return was both practical from a political standpoint and emotionally satisfying on a personal level.

Relationship to Investment

Gaining a firm understanding of your prospect's relationship to his investment includes multiple factors. They include what he considers a sizable *versus* a minor investment, what kind of time line he expects, and how he expects reporting to be done. Although this sounds like straightforward information collection, the reality is that people sometimes feel differently about these factors than their words would suggest. Your challenge is to pick up with the signals the prospect is unintentionally sending.

Maryann witnessed a colossal failure related to this second point; it's the opposite of managing the critical factor! She was hired as a consultant to a startup company in the medical technology field. Jed, the company founder, invited her to sit in on several meetings with potential investors so she could help him improve his presentation. The first prospect was a gentleman who belonged to the same country club as Jed. This fact had convinced Jed that the sell would be easy; he made an assumption that their common enjoyment of golf and their club would infuse the potential investor with a sense of trust. His attitude prevented him from doing any serious homework before the meeting about the man's current investments, and he didn't bother to ask him any questions about them during the meeting. He was flying blind, asking for a million dollars on the basis of tribal affiliation.

"I know you trust me to deliver," Jed told him. "And I will deliver! Within three years, you should see a four-to-one return on your money."

Maryann knew there was no reason for optimism when the potential investor got up from the small conference table and walked over to his desk. He sat down behind the desk and took out a piece of paper. Within a minute, he had drawn a series of squares on it. He drew a total of 36 squares on the page as she and Jed watched. The investor put "($1,000,000)" in the first square, signifying that he was in the hole one million dollars. He then put ditto marks in every other box, signifying that he was in the hole one million dollars for 36 months.

The investor's priorities included a time line as well as rate of return—something that Jed would have known if he looked at prospect's patterns of investment and had a conversation with him about what he considered a reasonable duration to tie up his money.

The investor's immediate use of a barrier to separate himself from the encounter, as well as the silence he used to put even more distance between himself and Jed, were clear signs the meeting should end immediately. But Jed persisted in his misperception that their common social experience would hold the conversation together so that he could prevail. The investor was visibly perturbed; a look of contempt on his face was combined with clasped hands on the desk, furthering shielding the prospect from Jed.

Knowing the meeting needed to end promptly, Maryann got up and thanked the gentleman for his time. Jed reluctantly got up and approached the desk, suggesting with his body language that he wanted to shake the man's hand. The investor's hands remained clasped and he did not get up to usher them out.

Signs of Moving Toward Acceptance

Earlier in the book, we covered the basic body language of acceptance. A number of indicators prior to actual acceptance tell you that you are on the right track.

Even before you see a genuine smile, you will notice the prospect directing his energy toward you. Good eye contact, active listening, and mirroring all indicate that your rapport is strengthening.

Movements like nods and leaning in will encourage you to keep talking. You will also see arms and posture conveying relaxation and connection. Part of the sense of openness is that barriers will be minimized or removed entirely. Once you and your product or service has been accepted, there is no need to maintain distance or barriers.

Summary Points

- ROI selling is number-based, but both "return" and "investment" can have non-monetary meanings. Whatever definition you use, ROI selling is never just about money; it's about human interaction.

- ROI selling is a subjective process even though ROI itself is a numbers-based concept.

- Something as innocent as giving an off-handed response to a question about maintenance costs, for example, can trigger the body language of deception.

- If you can spot the behavior of deception, you can do something to bring the discussion back to core agenda—that is, the money your customer will save or make as a result of doing business with you.

- A lie is something that is said, or not said, that alters a fact. Regardless of how reasonable the statement is, your body knows that what just came out of your mouth isn't consistent with what is in your head and/or heart—and your body will produce a stress response.

- Every part of a person's body tells a story about his or her emotional response to what you've done. In ROI selling, we are focused on stress, with signs of deception, so look forehead to feet.

- The characteristics of voice—tone, pitch, or pace—that a person uses to answer your questions are important if they are different from what you've heard before.

  You have won if you have managed the two critical factors:

  1. Getting the answer to the question "This is a good return relative to *what?*"

  2. Gaining a firm understanding of your prospect's relationship to his investment.

- When you think you have "won," look for confirmation in the body language of acceptance.

10

·········

FEAR SELLING

Fear selling leverages a prospect's feeling of vulnerability to draw the person toward your product, service, or idea. It is a powerful approach, but it needs to be used cautiously. If the technique is used toward the end of the meeting, the close occurs when the prospect feels as though the purchase is empowering. It replaces the feeling of vulnerability with a sense of control over the threat.

In the article "5 Best Cinematic Sales Pitches," *Inc.* magazine featured a corny opening to a 1962 movie musical as one of them. *Inc.* then pointed out how spot-on it is in the context of modern fear selling. First, the movie version.

In the scene, "Professor" Harold Hill is a con man trying to sell musical instruments to parents in a fictional Iowa town in 1912. His pitch is that he will prevent their sweet sons from turning into slackers and hoodlums by teaching them how to play music—something he has neither the ability nor intention to do. He's trying to plot a way with his old pal Marcellus to put the fear of God into the residents of River City so they fork over their money for his instruments.

Hill: I need some ideas if I'm going to get your town out of the serious trouble it's in!

Marcellus: River City ain't in any trouble.

Hill: Then I have to create some. Must create a desperate need in your town for a boys' band. (Sees people filing into the Pleez-All Billiard Parlor). So why does everyone keep rubbering into the billiard parlor?

Marcellus: Oh, they just got in a new pool table.

Hill: They must have seen a pool table before.

Marcellus: No. Just billiards.

Hill: That'll do it! (Runs to the Dunlop grocery store next to the billiard parlor and approaches the grocer). Are you Mr. Dunlop? Well, either you're closing your eyes to a situation you do not wish to acknowledge, or you are not aware of the caliber of disaster indicated by the presence of a pool table in your community!

With those words, he launches into "Ya' Got Trouble," the famous opening number from *The Music Man*. Of course, his solution to avert the degradation that will occur when boys spend their time at the pool table is to buy his musical instruments.

Inc. magazine followed the clip from the movie posted on its website with this observation: "He [Hill] begins his sales pitch by getting his potential customers to envision how horrible the future will be unless they buy his product. This is exactly how 'enterprise' computer companies pitch to top management. If Harold Hill were pitching ERP or CRM software today, he'd be singing that 'there's disruptive innovation in River City.'"[1]

One thing that Hill gets wrong—which is okay because he's a character in musical comedy—is that manufactured fears do not work in real-world fear selling. (The exception would be having prospects as gullible as the residents of River City.) A professional effectively using fear selling will point out an existing fear, demonstrate that he is knowledgeable about it and cares about the prospect's need to eradicate it, and then gives that person the means to do so. Fear selling brings with it a number of risks for a sales professional, however.

The Risks of Fear Selling

Fear selling takes advantage of a reality that most of us do not want to admit: A great many of us are more strongly motivated to avoid pain than to gain pleasure. In business terms, a threat to financial stability or data security, for example, is often a more powerful emotional driver in making a buying decision that one based on revenue opportunity.

Because a person who feels under siege in some way is emotionally charged, you have to be very careful with fear selling. Whether the encounter is between two people is a sales meeting, a negotiation, or a humanitarian plea, if one individual is fueled by emotion and the other is maintaining a rational approach, the latter person has the upper hand. The reason is that a person goes into limbic mode when emotions surge and that results in a loss of cognitive ability. A person in limbic mode is not functioning at her peak—not by a long shot.

If you move a prospect to make a buying decision while his judgment is affected by strong emotion, you run the risk of derailing your relationship with him. When he realizes that he authorized a major purchase while his judgment was impaired, he will feel as though he lost something instead of gaining it. He could very likely resent the experience and the outcome, and possibly regret his decision. Some or all of this negative response may not even be on a conscious level. All you know is that one day you try to schedule a follow-up meeting only to find that the person won't book an appointment with you.

Let's step back for a moment and get perspective on why people have such a profound response to the alleviation of a threat. A classic explanation comes from psychologist Abraham Maslow. In 1943, he introduced his theory on the hierarchy of needs. It includes five tiers, with the theory being that a person struggles to progress up the tiers until the needs of the lower tiers are met.

The ground floor is biological needs: food, sleep, sex, and other elements essential to life. One level up, you find the things and circumstances in life that provide safety; people have a profound need to be shielded from threats. Above that is the human requirement for belonging and connection. Here we are talking about family relationships, romantic involvements, a sense of team at work, and the unconditional love you get from your dog or cat. At the fourth level are esteem needs, such as achievement and reputation. The top tier of Maslow's hierarchy is self-actualization. People who have achieved and sustained self-actualization might include the Dalai Lama and a career nurse who finds great fulfillment in her work.

In the Maslow model, achievement and reputation can theoretically come only when someone feels as though he belongs. Similarly, the personal growth and fulfillment associated with self-actualization can only come after satisfying the need for achievement and reputation.

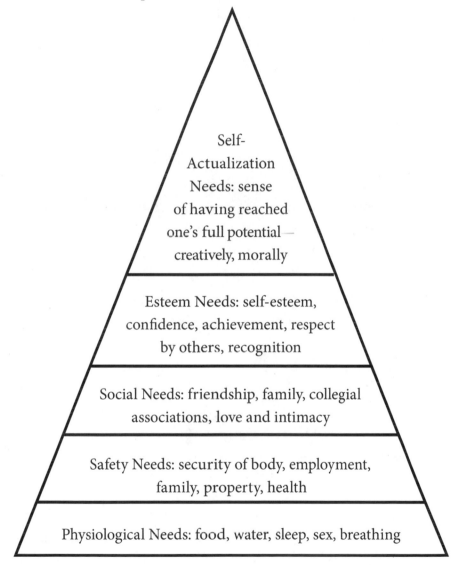

Maslow was more nuanced than any of these conclusions suggest, however, and the nuances make a difference in the context of our discussion of fear selling. In his famous paper, "A Theory in Human Motivation," Maslow wrote:

So far, our theoretical discussion may have given the impression that these five sets of needs are somehow in a step-wise, all-or-none relationships to each other. We have spoken in such terms as the following: "If one need is satisfied, then another emerges." This statement might give the false impression that a need must be satisfied 100 per cent before the next need emerges. In actual fact, most members of our society who are normal, are partially satisfied in all their basic needs and partially unsatisfied in all their basic needs at the same time.[2]

What is important for a sales professional to know, then, is that your relationship with the prospect or customer is just as important—if not more so—than the fear you are trying to allay. People can have fears and still seek and enjoy connections. The chances are good that the fear you trying to address for a customer is just one of many challenges and opportunities that she is facing in her professional life. If you focus too intently on the one issue that triggers fear, you may have a short-term win, but you will possibly have a long-term loss in the level of trust you want with the customer. Whenever possible, fear selling needs to be paired with relationship selling. It's vital that the customer perceive your awareness of the spectrum of her needs, challenges, and desires, rather than a laser-focus on a source of threat.

Another risk you take with fear selling is skepticism about your motive. You may have the most honest intentions possible about eliminating a threat to a customer's business, but consider the climate in which you are operating. Politicians, activists, advertisers, and a host of other loud and influential voices are spreading fear about everything from bed bugs to an environmental apocalypse to microscopic bacteria. Messages of fear are everywhere, and they fuel skepticism about the legitimacy of the issues as much as they fuel genuine concern about them.

Even if you've done excellent homework on the challenges your prospect faces, you probably do not know if you are walking into a meeting with someone who has been jaundiced by fear selling from politicians, activists, advertisers, or other salespeople. You could be in conversation with someone whose biggest, and rather antagonistic, question for you is "What do you stand to gain from scaring me?"

No matter what form the question takes, this is not one you want to sidestep. In other words, you do *not* want to give an answer like "Our product will prevent data loss potentially costing you...." That is nothing more than an attempt to brush the question aside, and you don't want to do that with someone whose behavior is affected by strong emotion. If you want to turn the corner, you need to give a direct answer to a direct question. Say something like, "I believe I have a solution for you and, yes, I will earn a commission on it."

In fear selling, never lose sight of the fact that you are leveraging emotions, but that those emotions need to be kept simmering and not boiling. In previous chapters, we covered the body language of positive and negative emotions. Use that to your advantage in understanding whether you are forging a better connection or creating distance from a prospect or customer.

Turning Fear Selling Into Relationship Selling

We can find countless examples of buyer's remorse after a fear sale in the world of consumer goods and they provide useful models of how to make the shift in B2B selling as well. Essentially, buyer's remorse is averted by shifting from a fear sale to a relationship sale.

In the consumer arena, many makers of skincare products know how to do this. If the target is young people, the ad opens with an attractive teen marred by bad skin. If the target is older women, there is a close-up of a face full of wrinkles. These images are the first phase of the fear approach, getting the viewers for whom this is relevant to stay tuned. They expect that what will follow is an explanation of what it will take to get rid of the unsightly condition. The ad meets the expectation by showing the same people with dramatically improved skin.

Then it's time for the second phase of fear selling. Viewers learn that unless they act fast, they will miss a great deal on this normally expensive product. The imperative is to call or go online immediately or the miracle cure for their skin condition will be costlier.

What many of these companies seemed to have learned is that getting the consumer to make that call is not nearly enough. It's easy to cancel a credit card purchase. To avert that, the companies quickly transition to relationship selling by expressing both concern and expertise in regular emails to the new customer: *"We are here if you have any questions!" "Here's a tip to make the product last longer!" "Do you have any suggestions to make our packaging better?"*

In the corporate environment, a comparable turn from fear to relationship selling could be a crucial part of a sales encounter on certain technology and support services. The fear sell is that, without what you have to offer, the prospect will spend too much money on IT infrastructure, not have the scalability to accommodate growth, and be faced with costly software upgrades in a year. But the customer brings his own set of fears to the table. He thinks what you're selling is more than he needs.

In other words, in your first meeting with a prospect, there could be a double-whammy of fear affecting the meeting: the fear you want to instill and the pre-existing fear that you want to dispel. Forget about closing a deal for now. Your primary goal for this meeting— at least in the beginning—is to inspire trust. You need to commit to building a relationship with this prospect before you try to focus him on the fear issues.

- Ask a non-pertinent question. To recap, this is a question that shows interest in the person or her situation. The purpose is to engage the person in a positive way, preferably about business but not about the subject at hand. You could say, "Congratulations on the move! How has everyone adjusted to the new headquarters location?"

- Maintain good eye contact. Show the prospect you are keenly interested in her answer.

- Keep your hands and arms open and relaxed. Don't cross your arms or grab a pen or interlace your fingers. You want to come across as centered, calm, and focused.

- Mirror the other person, but remember that does not mean mimic. A head lean, an arm position, a shared nod in agreement—movements like these should be subtle. They come naturally to most people when there is a genuine connection forming.

- Show you are friendly, not scary. Smile.

- Return to the fear-related issues that need to be addressed only after you see that your prospect's body language is much like your own: centered, calm, and focused. When you observe that, ask a good question, that is, a question that invites an explanation, description, or other narrative response. Listen well.

In shifting from fear selling to any other selling approach, you are managing change. Your ability to navigate your prospect's channels of thought, and to take him in directions he had not considered, is what a successful sales professional does. All the while, it's vital that you are able to read his body language to know when you are moving his thinking in your direction, and when he is pulling away.

People feel energized in a sales encounter when they feel they are in a position of authority and strength. They are not as afraid to trust. From your perspective in sales, you need to know if the customer stands to lose anything if the meeting goes the way you want (that is, you make the sale). As part of your conversation, try to ascertain if there are any potential negative repercussions as a result of his choosing your product or service. These might include:

- Having to defend the expenditure to a boss.

- Additional reporting requirements created by the purchase.

- Facing a performance review that includes an evaluation of the solution you just sold him.

- Protests from colleagues who wanted to go with a different vendor or solution.

The last thing you need is a customer going from a place of fear about a business issue to fear that the steps he's taken will provoke other threats!

Through your words and your body language, you want to engender the perception that your customer is strong and is on a path to "winning."

One of the pitfalls of fear selling is that removal of a threat and the accompanying sense of relief are not the same as winning. It's more like not losing—and that's a weak foundation for an ongoing relationship. With that in mind, you also need to be able to answer the question "What does winning mean for this customer?" Even though you thought you identified the issues causing him pain, you may still not have clarity on what constitutes a win for him. Ask questions until you two are speaking the same language about his needs and desires relative to the product or service you are offering. They will shed light on what he considers winning.

Finally, you make real progress with the customer when your conversation turns from solving a problem to identifying an opportunity. When you reach the point when your customer breaths a sign of relief that you have offered her what she needs to eliminate a threat, she's done looking backward. Now she's in the frame of mind to look forward.

Summary Points

- Fear selling is powerful, but needs to be used cautiously.

- When it works, fear selling replaces the customer's feeling of vulnerability with a sense of control over a threat.

- A big risk in fear selling that you are arousing emotions in your prospect. However, when emotions surge that results in a loss of cognitive ability. In other words, the buy might not be a fully rational choice for the person.

- If you move a prospect to make a buying decision while his judgment is affected by strong emotion, you run the risk of derailing your relationship with him.

- Another risk you take with fear selling is skepticism about your motive. It would be common for the prospect in a fear sale to wonder whose best interests you have at heart.

- In fear selling, you are leveraging emotions, but those emotions need to be kept simmering and not boiling.

- You run the risk of invoking buyer's remorse when fear is a central component of the sale. You can avert buyer's remorse by shifting from a fear sale to a relationship sale.

- In managing the change to a relationship sale, shift away the issues causing fear. Only return to the fear-related issues that need to be addressed after you see that your prospect's body language is much like your own: centered, calm, and focused.

- One of the pitfalls of fear selling is that removal of a threat is not the same as winning. Use your conversation to ferret out what your customer perceives as a "win."

PRACTICES AND EXERCISES

··········

MAKE THE SECRETS YOURS

A secret has allure because the information is guarded and known only to a chosen few. Now that you have been exposed to insights about reading and using movements, vocal characteristics, and appearance in the context of a sales encounter, do you know body language sales secrets? Not exactly. The big secret is how to turn this knowledge into a skill set.

We have composed a series of actions you can take throughout the day to put your knowledge into practice and make discoveries about body language. Aside from the first one, these are not activities you should feel the need to do daily. They are go-to training exercises to rely on when you want to spend a few minutes honing your skill set. The benefit is being able to use that skill set naturally in the context of sales encounters so that body language consistently works to your advantage.

Some of the exercises are self-focused, but that does not mean you do all of them alone. Some of them involve observing strangers; others invite you to scrutinize friends and colleagues. We hope you will at least do the exercises involving television and movies with other people. Differing interpretations of body language and vocal responses will lead to useful insights, both about the characters in the shows and about your friends! Remember that our interpretations of body language commonly reflect our projections of meanings due to your own background and experiences.

We conclude with some quick exercises on self-discovery, self-control, and self-direction. Reading other people offers you a big plus in sales encounters, but shaping how other people read you also has immeasurable benefits.

A Daily Practice in Using Body Language to Your Advantage

A number of practices in the realm of self-improvement are valuable to help you focus your energy, feel calm, and lift your spirits. They can help you continue to evolve as a sales professional. One practice that we find useful and were able to build on for you is part one of a two-step process developed by Tony Robbins that he calls "priming."

Try starting your day by setting aside 10 minutes in the morning for quiet reflection and breathing. Out of that will flow a one-minute exercise on body language that we designed.

During this time, spend the first three minutes thinking about three things you're grateful for. Spend the next three minutes feeling at peace and thinking of people you care about. And lastly, spend three minutes envisioning three things you want to accomplish.[1]

We recommend letting one of those three things you want to accomplish rise to the top. Identify three big emotions associated with it. For example, you have your first meeting with a potentially major client later that day and you want it be a success. The emotions you identify are joy, confidence, and determination. Get up with a lot of energy and put a genuine smile on your face. Stand up straight with your eyes focused forward. Stride across the room—that means walk forward in a deliberate manner with the smile still on your face. Your body is now communicating joy, confidence, and determination *to you*. If you can energize yourself to feel those emotions, then you can communicate them to other people!

To help you make the connection between certain actions and positive emotions, here is a sampling of movements (in alphabetical order, not order of importance) that you can refer to in preparation for doing the exercise:

Movement	Emotion You Feel or Want to Generate	Response From Others You Want to Cause
Arms behind the back with erect posture	Authority, supreme confidence	The kind of deference a military general gets
Arms up in a V-posture	Power, confidence, the thrill of victory	(This one is just for you, a "power move" to get psyched and centered.)
Arms wide	Satisfaction for a job well done	Praise and admiration
Arms/hands on hips	Dominance	Perceived confidence, deference

Movement	Emotion You Feel or Want to Generate	Response From Others You Want to Cause
Authoritarian stance (feet shoulder width apart; arms at side)	Confidence, preparedness for action, dominance	Perceived confidence, deference
Chest thrust	Dominance, strength	Deference
Erect posture	Confidence, pride, strength, dominance, competence	Respect and reliance on your abilities
Genuine smile	Joy, thrill, pleasure	Warmth and trust
Striding	Confidence, happiness, determination	Desire to move forward

Here are visual representations of selected movements.

The next sets of exercises can be done anytime and as often as you find them useful. Some involve working with another person, but you could also turn them into a "team sport" with multiple colleagues.

Exercises to Enhance Reading Others' Behavior

The first set of exercises invites you to observe people around you or recall the behavior of people you know. None of them is about engagement; you simply watch. After that, we ask you to watch again, but this time your observational skills are focused on people featured on either the little or the big screen. The only aspect of these exercises that would engage other people is interacting with, and learning from, the people who do the exercises with you.

Real People Around You

Go to a public place like a restaurant or shopping mall and observe real people using the Big Four: illustrators, regulators, adaptors, and barriers.

- Note how cultural and gender differences affect the expressiveness of the person.

- Look at the movements in conjunction with the facial expression. Do they match? Name the emotion you think is being expressed.

Go where you are likely to see people on a date, like a restaurant or a bar.

- Look for mirroring. People who want to be together will automatically start mirroring each other.

- Look for barriers and other signs of distancing. People who have reasons to hesitate about being together will use barriers. Sometimes they will push their chair or bar stool farther away from the person to increase the separation even more.

- Look for postures like the chest thrust or military stance described previously in which the man or woman is trying to be assertive. How is the other person responding?

Think of 10 people you have had repeated contact with in a business environment.

- How would you describe their dress and demeanor: rigid, put-together, casual, or negligent?

- Match the appearance with what you know about their behavior.

- What would you do differently with each of them in trying to influence their behavior? How might you—or do you—dress different or act differently in trying to persuade them to do what you want?

At an internal company meeting, where people are far more likely to be honest about their emotions than at a client meeting, try to detect stress.

- Jot down some notes of your perception of participants' baseline behaviors.

- Next to those notes, write down what you observe as deviations from baseline—that is, signs of stress no matter how minimal.

If writing notes makes it obvious that you are doing something other than listening to your colleagues, then just make mental notes.

Television and Movies

Watch television shows and videos with the purpose of connecting emotions with body language, spotting deception, and identifying conversation motivators.

Whether you are watching a scripted show or reality television, keep in mind that not all actors are created equal. You're learning what *not* to do (that is, bad acting) when you know that a person is trying to express a particular emotion, but the body language doesn't match. This can help you avoid being a "bad actor."

Connecting Emotions With Body Language

Unlike the people you observed in the mall, with a show you have context and conversation to inform you judgment about the emotions being conveyed.

- Turn off the sound. Given what you already know—or think you know—about the characters and how they feel about each other, are the illustrators and facial expressions effectively conveying emotions? If not, then are they bad actors, or are the characters perpetrating some kind of deception about how they feel?

- Turn the sound back on. How much does the tone of voice affect your conclusions about the emotions present?

Spotting Deception

Make a list of statements that you think are blatantly false or exaggerations. Make a note when it seems to you that some key information is missing—that is, you hear a lie of omission.

- Try it with both comedy and drama. With sitcoms, some kind of lie generally happens every couple of minutes since hyperbole is one of the standard techniques of comedy writing. In this exercise, log it as a lie.

- Rank the lie from one to three. One would be "It's barely a lie." Two is "Oh, come on. That can't be true." Three is "Obvious lie."

Identifying Conversation Motivators

Crime shows and legal dramas involving some kind of interrogation or cross-examination are prime candidates for this exercise.

- Your aim is first to spot the use of the eight conversation motivators we described: direct questioning, offering incentives, enhancing emotional appeal, boosting ego, deflating ego, easing fears, creating certainty or uncertainty, and silence.

- After you identify the use of a conversation motivator, pay attention to the effect it has on the other person.

This exercise focuses only on direct questions and the ways that people often avoid them. It is particularly applicable to politicians, but you will notice some of the same patterns of evasion with celebrities on late-night interview shows.

- Watch a press conference or an interview show with a politician, diplomat, or other person who is likely practiced with media interviews.

- Is the person giving direct answers to direct questions? That is, does he say yes or no in answering a yes-or-no question?

- Does the person evade the question to make it more palatable to answer? For example, "Senator, do you think California should secede from the United States?" The senator begins, "Well, I have always enjoyed the beaches in Southern California...."

- When the person evades a question, what body language do you see? Note also any changes in pitch, tone, or pace, and the use of other vocal characteristics that he is not quite comfortable with the question and/or the answer.

Exercises to Enhance Understanding Your Own Behavior

Just as you involved other people in determining your own baseline, involve people you trust in ascertaining your rituals related to emotion. Recruit a couple of people who have seen you in multiple circumstances and know what you're like when you experience certain feelings.

- How do you telegraph your anger? Have your friends or associates consider the full spectrum, from annoyed to furious. Recognize what you do from head to toe, such as scowling, putting your hands on your hips, clenching your teeth, and putting rigidity into your legs.

- What signals do you exhibit when you are nervous? Again, have the observations relate to the spectrum of mild tension to high anxiety. Consider not only your adaptors, but also the energy level in your illustrators, the degree to which you barrier and how you do it, and any other detectable displays of stress.

- How do you display defensiveness? This can be a tough one, but if you can nail it, then you have important information for your sales encounters. Regardless of what kind of selling you do, it is highly likely that you will feel defensive at some point. The more accurate you are in knowing how it shows up, the more you can control the expression of it.

Exercises to Elevate Your Skills

The two exercises in this section relate to stress responses and listening. You achieve a great deal—and have huge advantages in both professional and personal situations—if you can mute your expression of stress and amplify your ability to listen.

Managing Stress Responses

People typically have unique ways they ease discomfort in a new situation. You walk into a reception, sit down at an important meeting, or get in front of an audience of any size to deliver a presentation, and your body defaults to one or more actions to make you feel better. Do you clutch your glass, rub your fingers together, shuffle your feet, or do some other idiosyncratic gestures to make yourself feel better?

Be aware that you are entering a new situation and, whatever you' have determined to be your default response, *just don't do it.*

Sit still or stand still. Focus on someone else in the room. Ask a question and then just practice active listening.

Practicing Active Listening

Although listening is a skill that should come naturally to anyone who wants to have meaningful communication with another person, modern technology has made many people rusty. Short blasts of information substitute for conversation many times.

We have said it before and we will now say it the final time in this book: Listening is one of your most powerful skills in both connecting with and influencing people.

The first time you do this exercise, try it for just three minutes. Increase the time as much as you like when you repeat it.

- Choose a topic you know nothing about but the other person knows a lot about.

- Listen and learn. Ask questions to help yourself learn.

- Recount what you learned from the person at the end of the three minutes.

The next exercise is the opposite in an important way.

- Choose a topic you know a lot about—much more than the other person—and force yourself to listen without jumping in or correcting.

- During the three minutes, roughly how many times did you want to interrupt? How many times were you thinking, "That's totally off base!"?

In a situation like this, it's easy to prejudge what the other person is going to say and be wrong. It's also highly likely that the person will be wrong about a few things. The challenge is to wait until the person has finished speaking, and then figure out (a) which points really need to be addressed, and (b) how to express them in an informative rather than a critical way.

One more thing: Note well what your body was doing when you heard "bad" information coming from the other person.

•••••••••

We want to give you every possible advantage to achieve great success as a sales professional. Build on the information in the chapters and do the exercises.

What we have shared with you can be life-changing.

GLOSSARY

Active listening: listening with your whole body.

Adaptors: movements in response to anxiety.

Barriers: movements or use of objects to provide a shield.

Baseline: the composite of the movements and vocal expressions when you're in a relatively relaxed state.

Big Four: a term coined by Gregory Hartley (*The Art of Body Talk*) that refers to illustrators, regulators, adaptors, and barriers.

Comfort zone: a place where you feel unthreatened and in control.

Compound question: a question that combines two or more subjects, so you are essentially asking two questions at once.

Control question: a question to which you already know the answer.

Conversation motivators: techniques to get people talking.

Direct question: a question that leads with a basic interrogative.

Expertise selling: a sales interaction in which you differentiate yourself from other sales professionals by using your special knowledge and skills to meet a customer's needs.

Fear selling: a sales interaction in which you leverage a prospect's feeling of vulnerability to draw the person toward your product, service, or idea.

Haptics: the study of communication by touch.

Illustrators: movements that accentuate your message.

Incoming projection: projection that affects our perceptions.

Insight selling: a sales interaction in which your "solution" is recasting what was seen as a problem or guiding the customer in a different direction to discover new opportunities.

Leading question: a question suggesting the answer within the question.

Mirroring: a natural response to another person with whom you are interested in bonding; can be done intentionally to promote bonding.

Negative question: a question that integrates negatives such as "never" or "not" so that a person is unclear as to how to answer.

Non-pertinent question: a question that does not pertain to the subject you really want to discuss.

Outgoing projection: conveying how you want another person to respond to you.

Persistent question: a question that is repeated.

Regulators: movements that help control conversation.

Relationship selling: a sales interaction that focuses on the quality of exchange between you and the buyer rather than the price or specifications of the product or service.

Repeat question: a question that tries to uncover the same information as a previous question, but is different from the first one.

Return-on-investment (ROI) selling: a sales interaction in which you convince your prospects that you can improve their bottom line by increasing their profitability.

Solution selling: a sales interaction in which you satisfy customers by providing some combination of products and services that eliminates problems for them.

Summary question: a question that intended to allow the person to revisit a previous answer.

Visual accessing cues: unconscious eye movements when a person is thinking about something visual; eyes move toward the part of the brain responsible for vision—that is, the visual cortex, which is located in the back of the brain.

·········

NOTES

Chapter 2

1. Dr. Paul Eckman/Paul Eckman Group website, *www.paulekman.com/paul-ekman/*.

Chapter 3

1. From an April 27, 2014, interview with Elizabeth Bancroft for *Nothing but the Truth* by Maryann Karinch (Career Press, 2015), p. 67.

2. From an April 14, 2014, interview with Lena Sisco for *Nothing but the Truth* by Maryann Karinch (Career Press, 2015), p. 80.

3. Nick Morgan, "5 Tips for Presenting Boring Technical Information—So It Isn't Boring," *Forbes*, June 8, 2011,

www.forbes.com/sites/nickmorgan/2011/06/08/5-tips-for-presenting-boring-technical-information-so-it-isnt-boring/#7206060c5093.

4. Jason Nazar, "The 21 Principles of Persuasion," *Forbes,* May 26, 2013, *www.forbes.com/sites/jasonnazar/2013/03/26/the-21-principles-of-persuasion/#5f36b915a4c9.*

5. Paul Bloom and Deena Skolnick Weisberg, "Childhood Origins of Adult Resistance to Science," *Science* Vol. 316, Issue 5827 (May 18, 2007): 996–997; DOI: 10.1126/science.133398: *http://science.sciencemag.org/content/316/5827/996.full.*

6. Art Markman, PhD, "Do You Prefer More Choices or Less? It Depends on Distance," *Psychology Today,* February 5, 2013, *www.psychologytoday.com/log/ulterior-motives/201302/do-you-prefer-more-choice-or-less-it-depends-distance.*

Chapter 4

1. George Loewenstein, "The Psychology of Curiosity: A Review and Reinterpretation," *Psychological Bulletin* Vol. 116, No. 1 (1994): 75–98, *www.cmu.edu/dietrich/sds/docs/loewenstein/PsychofCuriosity.pdf.*

2. "Micro Expressions," Dr. Paul Eckman/Paul Eckman Group website, *www.paulekman.com/micro-expressions/.*

3. "President Obama Press Conference (August 9, 2013) [1/4]," 15:00, Posted by Definitely, August 9, 2013, *www.youtube.com/watch?v=BN0SHcrqTaI.*

4. Custom Development Solutions website, *www.cdsfunds.com/articles.html/.*

5. Piercarlo Valdesolo, "Flattery Will Get You Far," *Scientific American,* January 12, 2010, *www.scientificamerican.com/article/flattery-will-get-you-far/.*

6. Maryann Karinch, *Nothing but the Truth* (Career Press, 2015), p. 118.

Chapter 5

1. "Non Verbal Body Language Dictionary: D," Body Language Project website, *www.bodylanguageproject.com/dictionary/?s=disdain.*

Chapter 6

1. Polly Campbell, "The Selfish Act of Kindness," *Psychology Today,* December 17, 2009, *www.psychologytoday.com/blog/imperfect-spirituality/200912/the-selfish-act-kindness.*

2. Kate Taylor, "Here's the Letter Whole Foods Just Sent its Customers Who Are Furious About it 'Selling Out'," *Business Insider* June 16, 2017, *www.businessinsider.com/whole-foods-sends-letter-to-shoppers-after-amazon-backlash-2017-6.*

3. "The 100 Largest US Charities," *Forbes,* 2016, *www.forbes.com/companies/ymca/.*

4. "The Citadel's Mission Statement," The Citadel website, *www.citadel.edu/root/mission-statement.*

5. Ron Gutman, "The Hidden Power of Smiling," TED2011, March 2011, *www.ted.com/talks/ron_gutman_the_hidden_power_of_smiling.*

Chapter 7

1. Maryann Karinch, *Telemedicine: What the Future Holds When You're Ill* (Liberty Corner, N.J.: New Horizon Press, 1994).

2. From Now On website, *www.fno.org.*

3. Paul J. Zak, "The Neuroscience of Trust," *Harvard Business Review*, January–February 2017.

Chapter 8

1. Nicholas Toman, Brent Adamson, and Cristina Gomez, "The New Sales Imperative," *Harvard Business Review*, March–April 2017, *https://hbr.org/2017/03/the-new-sales-imperative.*

2. "Breathing Techniques," COPD Foundation website, *www.copdfoundation.org/What-is-COPD/Living-with-COPD/Breathing-Techniques.aspx.*

3. Paul Smith, *Sell With a Story: How to Capture Attention, Build Trust, and Close the Sale* (AMACOM, 2017), pp. 15–24.

Chapter 9

1. Peter Friedman, "5 Types of Social ROI With Big Business Impact," CMO, November 4, 2014, *www.cmo.com/features/articles/2014/10/22/five_types_of_social.html#gs.m=u6Qrw*

2. Ibid.

3. Ibid.

Chapter 10

1. Geoffrey James, "5 Best Cinematic Sales Pitches," *Inc.*, *www.inc.com/geoffrey-james/the-5-best-cinematic-sales-pitches.html.*

2. A.H. Maslow (1943), "A Theory of Human Motivation," *Psychological Review*, 50, 370-396, as presented in Classics in the History of Psychology, *http://psychclassics.yorku.ca/Maslow/motivation.htm.*

Practices and Exercises

1. Marguerite Ward, "Tony Robbins Shares a 2-Step Strategy for Feeling More in Control of Your Life," CNBC, July 22, 2017, *www.cnbc.com/2017/07/22/tony-robbins-shares-a-2-step-strategy-for-feeling-more-in-control-of-your-life.html.*

INDEX